The Complete

CONSTITUTION

OF THE

UNITED STATES OF AMERICA

Special Edition

Complete Index

History of The Constitutional Convention

Edited By William J. Murray

First Edition — 1987
Second Edition — 1999
Copyright 1987: MFM PUBLISHING

M F M
PUBLISHING

906 LAFAYETTE BLVD.
FREDERICKSBURG, VA 22401

THE COMPLETE CONSTITUTION
OF THE UNITED STATES OF AMERICA

CONTENTS

	Page
Foreword	V
A Young Nation Near Collapse	1
The Constitutional Convention	4
Ratification	9
The Constitution	10
Constitutional Cross Index	27
The Great Seal	74

"Proclaim liberty throughout all the land unto all the inhabitants thereof."
Leviticus 25:10

FOREWORD

In June of 1982 I was asked to speak on the issue of 'prayer in school' at a fund raising dinner for a private Christian school in Pennsylvania. The director of the school asked me to include some quotes from the founding fathers so their views of this Constitutional issue would be explored.

Because of my family's involvement in the removal of prayer from the public schools of the United States in 1963 I felt qualified to prepare such a lecture.[1]

The night of the dinner I arose and began to deliver my address. My message concerned the intention of the founding fathers in drafting the Constitution. Their intention being that the people of the United States should have representatives who prepare laws on their behalf rather than rulers who mandate laws.

Within minutes it became apparent to me that my audience had no earthly idea what I was talking about.

I stopped my lecture and asked the group of some 500 persons present this question: "How many of you have a copy of the U.S. Constitution in your home which you could check to see if what I am saying is correct?"

Of the group of 500 just 22 or less than 5% raised their hands. Astonished I pleaded for others who thought perhaps they had one somewhere to raise their hands. None did.

I then asked how many had ever heard of the Federalist Papers.[2] Less than 10 raised their hands.

At that very moment a great fear for our republic overwhelmed me. I cannot begin to express fully the emotions which went through me as I realized the great danger of ignorance I had discovered.

Ignorance is the downfall of nations. It is the ignorance of the people of the institutions of government which ultimately allows those institutions to dominate them.

It was then I decided to provide copies of the U.S. Constitution to people throughout the country.

I learned the U.S. Government Book Store in Dallas sold a small pocket size edition of the U.S. Constitution for $4.00. I purchased it and took it in to my printer. He could not control his laughter when I told him the little pocket size 28 page booklet was sold for $4.00 by the U.S. Government. His commet was, "Boy, they don't want to sell many of these." He was right.

So, in late 1982 I began to print and distribute copies of the Constitution of the United States of America. At first I printed no price on them and asked no specific amount for them at my various speaking engagements. That is until I realized how much money I was losing!

Remember that no man has ever died in combat for a President or a Senator. Nor has any of our servicemen died in combat for the flag or for a state. Every man who has ever given his life has done so to uphold the Constitution of the United States. That is each serviceman's sworn duty.

I was dumbfounded after six months of accepted 'contributions' for the Constitution to realize I was receiving an average of only 17 cents each. Upon that realization my fear for the republic grew.

Here was the document hundreds of thousands of men had died defending and today's American thought it was worth less than a quarter.

It was then I began in earnest to get what I believe is the world's most important document into the hands of the people of the United States.

I set up a small publishing company and began to wholesale the pocket editions of the Constitution to the nation's 10,000 plus book stores.

Between 1982 and 1987 this small publishing company has become the largest publisher of the U.S. Constitution. Our annual sales of the Constitution is into the hundred of thousands.

Yet in 1987 as we mark the 200th year of the Constitution less than 5% of the adults of this nation have a copy of the U.S. Constitution in their home.

It is my hope and my prayer that this year of celebration of the bicentennial of the Constitution will make more Americans than ever aware of the Constitution and its meaning to us.

The Constitution does not govern us as some believe. It guarantees us the right to govern ourselves. Let us all cherish it on this its 200th birthday.

William J. Murray
Publisher

---

[1] Murray vs. Curlett, Supreme Court of the United States, June 17th, 1963.

[2] A series of newspaper articles written by Hamilton, Madison and Jay to explain and promote the new Constitution during the ratification period from 1787 to 1788.

A YOUNG NATION NEAR COLLAPSE

John Adams

"Our Constitution was made only for a Moral and religious people. It is wholly inadequate to the government of any other." [1]

John Adams

A YOUNG NATION NEAR COLLAPSE

At noon on October 19th, 1781, the British Army of General Cornwallis surrendered to General George Washington on the battlefield at Yorktown, Virginia. Cornwallis and his army might have escaped the humiliating defeat at Yorktown by crossing the York River at Gloucester. However, as his men boarded the boats a huge wind and thunderstorm erupted forcing the fleet of escaping boats back to the Yorktown shore.

Cornwallis watching the escape being foiled by the storm proclaimed that God must be on the side of Washington.[2]

When news reached Britain of the surrender of Cornwallis it had a devastating moral effect on the nation. The will to fight American independence had vanished.

A preliminary peace treaty was signed on November 30th, 1782. The final treaty of peace was signed between Britain and the United States on February 3rd, 1783.

The young nation was far from being at peace with itself. Descent and turmoil were earmarks of the aftermath of the victory at Yorktown.

One faction led by the military wanted to proclaim a monarchy and favored George Washington to be its first king. Colonel Lewis Nicola, in a letter to Washington outlining the abuses heaped on the Army by the Congress, urged him to declare himself George I. Nicola's letter of May, 1782, assured General Washington of the support of the Army. Washington rejected the idea as a betrayal of the revolution.

In March of 1783 a letter was circulated within the Army calling for a military revolt and the establishment of a military government with Washington as its head. Washington called his officers together and denounced the plan.

In June of 1783 over 100 soldiers of the Pennsylvania line invaded the halls of Congress in Philadelphia and forced assembled Congress to flee for their lives. Never again was Congress convened in Philadelphia.

There was widespread economic depression and inflation caused by the issuance of worthless paper currency by the Continental Congress.

Heavy taxes approaching those of King George caused Shays' Rebellion. Shays gathered an army of some 1,100 men and attacked Springfield, Massachusetts in January of 1787. His army met defeat on January 24th, 1787.

There were also the intellectuals who proposed the new nation follow a path of economics called leveling. (Referred to in the 20th century as socialism.) Other Utopian dreamers proposed communism before Marx was ever born. It was an American idea called "community of goods" in which the state owned and operated all property and business for the good of the people.

Samual Adams later made this statement about those individuals: "The utopian schemes of leveling and a community of goods are as visionary and impracticable as those which vest all property in the Crown. These ideas are arbitrary, despotic, and, in our government, unconstitutional."[3]

The various states refused to pay their debts. The Army was unpaid. The widows of those who had fought received no pensions. Shopkeepers were paid off with inflated currency.

So bad was the national situation that Alexander Hamilton was led to say, "We may indeed with propriety be said to have reached almost the last stage of national humiliation. There is scarcely anything that can wound the pride or degrade the character of an independent nation which we do not experience."[4]

Alexander Hamilton called for a constitutional convention beginning in 1782. His call fell upon deaf ears until a trade conference during September of 1786 in Annapolis, Maryland. At that conference he drafted a call to amend the old Articles of Confederation to give Congress the power to deal with the problems of the new nation.

It was not until February 21st of 1787 that Congress agreed to call for a meeting of representatives of the various states ". . . for the sole and express purpose of revising the Articles of Confederation."

What followed was a miracle.

[1]John Hall, *The Changing Political Thought of John Adams* (Princetown, NJ: Princetown Univ. Press, 1966, p. 189.

[2]W. Cleon Skousen, *The Making of America*, (Washington, DC, The National Center For Constitutional Studies): p. 104.

[3]William V. Wells, *The Life and Public Service of Samuel Adams*, 3 vols., (Boston: Little, Brown & Co., 1865), vol. 1, p. 154.

[4]*Federalist Papers*, Number 15

THE CONSTITUTIONAL CONVENTION

Benjamin Franklin

Benjamin Franklin was 81 years old and President (or Governor) of Pennsylvania at the time of the constitutional convention in 1787.

"Only a virtuous people are capable of freedom. As nations become corrupt and vicious, they have more need of masters." [1]

Benjamin Franklin

The Continental Congress had called the special delegates from the various states to meet in Philadelphia on May 14th, 1787.

The young nation was in depression and crumbling. Yet, despite the urgency of the meeting, many of the states failed to pay even the transportation costs of their delegates. James Madison, who was later to become one of our presidents, was forced to borrow money to attend.

George Washington made the ride despite his arm being in a sling from a painful case of rheumatism. Of the 73 delegates who had been appointed by the states only 55 showed up. Most of those were late and the actual convention did not get under way until May 25th, 1787.

The make-up of those present was varied. Their backgrounds gave the convention as a whole an unusually good understanding of the needs of a new nation.

Of the 55 delegates 28 had previously served in Congress. Seventeen of the delegates had served as officers during the Revolution. Of those 4 had served on the staff of General Washington. Three were college professors and 2 had been college presidents.

The majority of the delegates were lawyers. Thirty-one belonged to that profession and several had served as judges.

On the whole the delegates to the Constitutional Convention were young. Only 1 man, Benjamin Franklin was past 60. He had celebrated his 81st birthday. The average age of the group was 41 and several of the delegates were under 30.

James Madison continued with the argument he had begun in 1782, that no amount of patch work could save the Articles of Confederation.

Madison prevailed.

When the convention was officially opened on May 25th George Washington was unanimously elected as the president of the convention. Major William Jackson was elected as secretary.

The rules of the convention were readily adopted and agreed to. They were:

1. All meetings were to be held in secret.
2. Each state was to have only one vote on each issue to be determined by majority vote of the delegates of the state.
3. No delegate could speak more than twice on a single issue. (Unless all delegates had received an opportunity to speak on the issue.)
4. All remarks had to be addressed to the President of the convention, George Washington. (This avoided floor arguments between members.)

Between May 25th and June 19th the constitutional convention moved swiftly. Much of the "Virginia Plan" presented by Governor Edmund Randolpf on May 29th was approved in one form or another. By the end of this period only three major issues remained on which no agreement could be reached.

The three main points of contention among the delegates were:

1. Representation of states in the new Congress.

2. Regulation of trade by the new federal government.

3. The issue of slavery.

The smaller and less populated states wanted a system of representation in which each state had an equal vote. The larger and more populous states desired proportionate representation based on the population of each state.

Those states which were industrial giants wanted free trade between states and overseas. Those states not endowed with large industries wanted the right to tax imports.

The southern, predominantly agricultural states, including Virginia, wanted the new constitution to protect the institution of slavery. The industrial states of the North, seeking cheap labor, wanted an end to slavery.

The Virginia plan was the cradle in which the Constitution was born, yet it was that state which stood by slavery.

Between June 19th and July 26th the delegates wrestled with these problems. At one point George Washington was in such distress that he wrote, "I almost despair of seeing a favorable issue to the proceedings of the Convention, and do therefore repent having had any agency in the business." [2]

It was during this period of crisis on June 28th that Benjamin Franklin gave his now famous and much quoted plea for prayer within the chambers of the convention. He said:

"In the beginning of the contest with Britain, when we were sensible of danger, we had daily prayers in this room for divine protection. Our prayers, sir, were heard; and they were graciously answered. All of us who were engaged in the struggle must have observed frequent instances of a superintending Providence in our favor. To that kind Providence we owe this happy opportunity of consulting in peace on the means of establishing our future national felicity. And have we now forgotten that powerful Friend? Or do we imagine that we no longer need assistance?

"I have lived, sir, a long time; and the longer I live the more convincing proofs I see of this truth: that God governs the affairs of men. And if a sparrow cannot fall to the ground without His notice, is it probable that an empire can rise without His aid? We have been assured, sir, in the sacred writings, that 'except the Lord build the house they labor in vain that built it.' I firmly believe this; and I also believe that without His concurring aid we shall succeed in this political building no better than the builders of Babel; we shall be divided by our little partial, local interests, our projects will be confounded and we ourselves shall become a reproach and a byword down to future ages. And, what is worse, mankind may hereafter, from this unfortunate instance, despair of establishing government by human wisdom and leave it to chance, war, or conquest.

"I, therefore, beg leave to move:

"That hereafter prayers, imploring the assistance of Heaven and its blessing on our deliberations, be held in this assembly every morning before we proceed to business, and that one or more of the clergy of this city be requested to officiate in that service."[3]

Franklin's call for divine help had a sobering influence on the convention. That same day Roger Sherman and Oliver Ellsworth of Connecticut offered a solution to the most troublesome problem facing the delegates. His plan called for a compromise between the big and small states on the issue of representation in Congress. The plan gave each state equal representation in the Senate, but proportional representation in the House of Representatives.

Since both the Senate and House had to pass a bill for it to become a law the smaller states saw this as a safeguard. However one final demand was made by the smaller states. They pushed for a specific article of the Constitution which would state that no amendment could ever be made to equal representation of the states in the Senate. Such was provided for in Article V, Section 1:

"No amendment to the Constitution can deprive the states of
equal representation and equal voting rights in the Senate."

Thus the smaller states were protected from populous centers taking over and centralizing control of the federal government.

By September 8th the Constitution was completed and given to a lawyer and professional writer from Pennsylvania, Gouverneur Morris. He and the Committee on Style did the final rewrite. It was approved by the delegates as a whole and given to a calligrapher to be inscribed.

On September 17th of 1787 the final document was presented to the 41 of the original 55 delegates who had remained throughout the proceedings. The signing of the document occurred in the east wing room of Independence Hall. At the request of Benjamin Franklin the majority of the delegates from each state signed. Three remaining delegates refused to sign. George Washington signed as president of the convention and delegate from Virginia.

What emerged from nearly four months of debate was the most unique political document ever. It was a true compromise of totally differing points of view on many substantial issues. It also brought our nation together.

Under the Articles of Confederation there was no executive branch and Congress ran the day to day affairs of the nation by committee. The Constitution provided for a separation of powers. A system of checks and balances which has stood the test of time for 200 years.

[1]Albert Smyth, *The Writings of Benjamin Franklin*, 10 vols. (New York: MacMillan Co., 1907), vol. 9, p. 569.

[2]John Fitzpatrick, *The Writings of George Washington*, 39 vols. (Washington, D.C.: U.S. Government Printing Office, 1931-44), vol. 29, p. 245.

[3]Smyth, *The Writings of Benjamin Franklin*, vol. 9, pp. 600-601.

George Washington

General George Washington signed the new Constitution as President and deputy from Virginia.

RATIFICATION

On December 6th, 1787, Delaware became the first state to ratify the Constitution. The Constitution became operational on June 21, 1788, when it was ratified by New Hampshire. Under the provisions of Article VII the Constitution went into effect when ratified by the 9th state.

The remaining 11 states ratified the Constitution on the following dates:

Pennsylvania	December 12th, 1787
New Jersey	December 18th, 1787
Georgia	January 2nd, 1788
Connecticut	January 9th, 1788
Massachusetts	February 6th, 1788
Maryland	April 26th, 1788
South Carolina	May 23rd, 1788
Virginia	June 26th, 1788
New York	July 26th, 1788
North Carolina	November 21, 1789
Rhode Island	May 29th, 1790

THE CONSTITUTION
OF THE
UNITED STATES

We the People of the United States, in Order to form a more perfect Union, establish Justice, insure domestic Tranquility, provide for the common defence, promote the general Welfare, and secure the Blessings of Liberty to ourselves and our Posterity, do ordain and establish this Constitution for the United States of America.

ARTICLE I.

SECTION I. All legislative Powers herein granted shall be vested in a Congress of the United States, which shall consist of a Senate and House of Representatives.

SECTION 2. The House of Representatives shall be composed of Members chosen every second Year by the People of the several States, and the Electors in each State shall have the Qualifications requisite for Electors of the most numerous Branch of the State Legislature.

No Person shall be a Representative who shall not have attained to the Age of twenty-five Years, and been seven Years a Citizen of the United States, and who shall not, when elected, be an Inhabitant of that State in which he shall be chosen.

[Representatives and direct Taxes shall be apportioned among the several States which may be included within this Union, according to their respective Numbers, which shall be determined by adding to the whole Number of free Persons, including those bound to Service for a Term of Years, and excluding Indians not taxed, three fifths of all other Persons.]* The actual Enumeration shall be made within three Years after the first Meeting of the Congress of the United States, and within every subsequent Term of ten Years, in such Manner as they shall by Law direct. The Number of Representatives shall not exceed one for every thirty Thousand,** but each State shall have at Least one Representative; and until such enumeration shall be made, the State of New Hampshire shall be entitled to chuse three, Massachusetts eight, Rhode-Island and Providence Plantations one, Connecticut five, New-York six, New Jersey four, Pennsylvania eight, Delaware one, Maryland six, Virginia ten, North Carolina five, South Carolina five, and Georgia three.

[NOTE: This booklet presents the Constitution and all amendments in their original form. Items which have since been amended or superseded, as identified in the footnotes, are bracketed.]

*Changed by section 2 of the fourteenth amendment.
**Ratio in 1965 was one to over 410,000.

When vacancies happen in the Representation from any State, the Executive Authority thereof shall issue Writs of Election to fill such Vacancies.

The House of Representatives shall chuse their Speaker and other Officers; and shall have the sole Power of Impeachment.

SECTION 3. The Senate of the United States shall be composed of two Senators from each State, [chosen by the Legislature thereof,]*** for six Years; and each Senator shall have one Vote.

Immediately after they shall be assembled in Consequence of the first Election, they shall be divided as equally as may be into three Classes. The Seats of the Senators of the first Class shall be vacated at the Expiration of the second Year, of the second Class at the Expiration of the fourth Year, and of the third Class at the Expiration of the sixth Year, so that one-third may be chosen every second Year; [and if Vacancies happen by Resignation, or otherwise, during the Recess of the Legislature of any State, the Executive thereof may make temporary Appointments until the next Meeting of the Legislature, which shall then fill such Vacancies.]*

No Person shall be a Senator who shall not have attained to the Age of thirty Years, and been nine Years a Citizen of the United States, and who shall not, when elected, be an Inhabitant of that State for which he shall be chosen.

The Vice President of the United States shall be President of the Senate, but shall have no Vote, unless they be equally divided.

The Senate shall chuse their other Officers, and also a President pro tempore, in the absence of the Vice President, or when he shall exercise the Office of President of the United States.

The Senate shall have the sole Power to try all Impeachments. When sitting for that Purpose, they shall be on Oath or Affirmation. When the President of the United States is tried, the Chief Justice shall preside: And no Person shall be convicted without the Concurrence of two thirds of the Members present.

Judgment in Cases of Impeachment shall not extend further than to removal from Office, and disqualification to hold and enjoy any Office of honor, Trust or Profit under the United States: but the Party convicted shall nevertheless be liable and subject to Indictment, Trial, Judgment and Punishment, according to Law.

SECTION 4. The Times, Places and Manner of holding Elections for Senators and Representatives, shall be prescribed in each State by the Legislature thereof; but the Congress may at any time by Law make or alter such Regulations, except as to the Place of Chusing Senators.

The Congress shall assemble at least once in every Year, and such Meeting shall [be on the first Monday in December,]** unless they shall by Law appoint a different Day.

SECTION 5. Each House shall be the Judge of the Elections, Returns and Qualifications of its own Members, and a Majority of each shall constitute a Quorum to do Business; but a smaller number may adjourn from day to day, and may be authorized to compel the Attendance of absent Members, in such Manner, and under such Penalties as each House may provide.

Each House may determine the Rules of its Proceedings, punish its Members for disorderly Behavior, and, with the Concurrence of two thirds, expel a Member.

***Changed by section 1 of the seventeenth amendment.

*Changed by clause 2 of the seventeenth amendment.

**Changed by section 2 of the twentieth amendment.

Each House shall keep a Journal of its Proceedings, and from time to time publish the same, excepting such Parts as may in their Judgment require Secrecy; and the Yeas and Nays of the Members of either House on any question shall, at the Desire of one fifth of those Present, be entered on the Journal.

Neither House, during the Session of Congress, shall, without the Consent of the other, adjourn for more than three days, nor to any other Place than that in which the two Houses shall be sitting.

SECTION 6. The Senators and Represenatives shall receive a Compensation for their Services, to be ascertained by Law, and paid out of the Treasury of the United States. They shall in all Cases, except Treason, Felony and Breach of the Peace, be privileged from Arrest during their Attendance at the Session of their respective Houses, and in going to and returning from the same; and for any Speech or Debate in either House, they shall not be questioned in any other Place.

No Senator or Representative shall, during the Time for which he was elected, be appointed to any civil Office under the Authority of the United States, which shall have been created, or the Emoluments whereof shall have been encreased during such time; and no Person holding any Office under the United States, shall be a Member of either House during his Continuance in Office.

SECTION 7. All Bills for raising Revenue shall originate in the House of Representatives; but the Senate may propose or concur with Amendments as on other Bills.

Every Bill which shall have passed the House of Representatives and the Senate, shall, before it become a Law, be presented to the President of the United States; If he approve he shall sign it, but if not he shall return it, with his Objections to that House in which it shall have originated, who shall enter the Objections at large on their Journal, and proceed to reconsider it. If after such Reconsideration two thirds of that House shall agree to pass the Bill, it shall be sent, together with the Objections, to the other House, by which it shall likewise to reconsidered, and if approved by two thirds of that House, it shall become a Law. But in all such Cases the Votes of both Houses shall be determined by Yeas and Nays, and the Names of the Persons voting for and against the Bill shall be entered on the Journal of each House respectively. If any Bill shall not be returned by the President within ten Days (Sundays excepted) after it shall have been presented to him, the Same shall be a Law, in like Manner as if he had signed it, unless the Congress by their Adjournment prevent its Return, in which Case it shall not be a Law.

Every Order, Resolution, or Vote to which the Concurrence of the Senate and House of Representatives may be necessary (except on a question of Adjournment) shall be presented to the President of the United States; and before the Same shall take Effect, shall be approved by him, or being disapproved by him, shall be repassed by two thirds of the Senate and House of Representatives, according to the Rules and Limitations prescribed in the Case of a Bill.

SECTION 8. The Congress shall have Power To lay and collect Taxes, Duties, Imposts and Excises, to pay the Debts and provide for the common Defence and general Welfare of the United States; but all Duties, Imposts and Excises shall be uniform throughout the United States;

To borrow money on the credit of the United States;

To regulate Commerce with foreign Nations, and among the several States, and with the Indian Tribes;

To establish an uniform Rule of Naturalization, and uniform Laws on the subject of Bankruptcies throughout the United States;

To coin Money, regulate the Value thereof, and of foreign Coin, and fix the Standard of Weights and Measures;

To provide for the Punishment of counterfeiting the Securities and current Coin of the United States;

To establish Post Offices and post Roads;

To promote the Progress of Science and useful Arts, by securing for limited Times to Authors and Inventors the exclusive Right to their respective Writings and Discoveries;

To constitute Tribunals inferior to the supreme Court;

To define and punish Piracies and Felonies committed on the high Seas, and Offenses against the Law of Nations;

To declare War, grant Letters of Marque and Reprisal, and make Rules concerning Captures on Land and Water;

To raise and support Armies, but no Appropriation of Money to that Use shall be for a longer Term than two Years;

To provide and maintain a Navy;

To make Rules for the Government and Regulation of the land and naval Forces;

To provide for calling forth the Militia to execute the Laws of the Union, supress Insurrections and repel Invastions;

To provide for organizing, arming, and disciplining the Militia, and for governing such Part of them as may be employed in the Service of the United States, reserving to the States respectively, the Appointment of the Officers, and the Authority of training the Militia according to the discipline prescribed by Congress;

To exercise exclusive Legislation in all Cases whatsoever, over such District (not exceeding ten Miles square) as may, by Cession of particular States, and the acceptance of Congress, become the Seat of the Government of the United States, and to exercise like Authority over all Places purchased by the Consent of the Legislature of the State in which the Same shall be, for the Erection of Forts, Magazines, Arsenals, dock-Yards, and other needful Buildings;—And

To make all Laws which shall be necessary and proper for carrying into Execution the foregoing Powers, and all other Powers vested by this Constitution in the Government of the United States, or in any Department or Officer thereof.

SECTION 9. The Migration or Importation of such Persons as any of the States now existing shall think proper to admit, shall not be prohibited by the Congress prior to the Year one thousand eight hundred and eight, but a tax or duty may be imposed on such Importation, not exceeding ten dollars for each Person.

The privilege of the Writ of Habeas Corpus shall not be suspended, unless when in Cases or Rebellion or Invasion the public Safety may require it.

No Bill of Attainder or ex post facto Law shall be passed.

No capitation, or other direct, Tax shall be laid, unless in Proportion to the Census or Enumeration herein before directed to be taken.*

No Tax or Duty shall be laid on Articles exported from any State.

No Preference shall be given by any Regulation of Commerce or Revenue to the Ports of one State over those of another: nor shall Vessels bound to, or from, one State, be obliged to enter, clear, or pay Duties in another.

No Money shall be drawn from the Treasury, but in Consequence of Appropriations made by Law; and a regular Statement and Account of the

*But see the sixteenth amendment.

Receipts and Expenditures of all public Money shall be published from time to time.

No Title of Nobility shall be granted by the United States: And no Person holding any Office of Profit or Trust under them, shall, without the Consent of the Congress, accept of any present, Emolument, Office, or Title, of any kind whatever, from any King, Prince, or foreign State.

SECTION 10. No State shall enter into any Treaty, Alliance, or Confederation; grant Letters of Marque and Reprisal; coin Money; emit Bills of Credit; make any Thing but gold and silver Coin a Tender in Payment of Debts; pass any Bill of Attainder, ex post facto Law, or Law impairing the Obligation of Contracts, or grant any Title of Nobility.

No State shall, without the Consent of the Congress, lay any Imposts or Duties on Imports or Exports, except what may be absolutely necessary for executing its inspection Laws: and the net Produce of all Duties and Imposts, laid by any State on Imports or Exports, shall be for the Use of the Treasury of the United States; and all such Laws shall be subject to the Revision and Controul of the Congress.

No State shall, without the Consent of Congress, lay any duty of Tonnage, keep Troops, or Ships of War in time of Peace, enter into any Agreement or Compact with another State, or with a foreign Power, or engage in War, unless actually invaded, or in such imminent Danger as will not admit of delay.

ARTICLE II.

SECTION I. The executive Power shall be vested in a President of the United States of America. He shall hold his Office during the Term of four Years, and, together with the Vice-President, chosen for the same Term, be elected, as follows.

Each State shall appoint, in such Manner as the Legislature thereof may direct, a Number of Electors, equal to the whole Number of Senators and Represenatives to which the State may be entitled in the Congress: but no Senator or Representative, or Person holding an Office of Trust or Profit under the United States, shall be appointed an Elector.

[The Electors shall meet in their respective States, and vote by Ballot for two persons, of whom one at least shall not be an Inhabitant of the same State with themselves. And they shall make a List of all the Persons voted for, and of the Number of Votes for each; which List they shall sign and certify, and transmit sealed to the Seat of the Government of the United States, directed to the President of the Senate. The President of the Senate shall, in the Presence of the Senate and House of Representatives, open all the Certificates, and the Votes shall then be counted. The Person having the greatest Number of Votes shall be the President, if such Number be a Majority of the whole Number of Electors appointed; and if there be more than one who have such Majority, and have an equal Number of Votes, then the House of Representatives shall immediately chuse by Ballot one of them for President; and if no Person have a Majority, then from the five highest on the List the said House shall in like Manner chuse the President. But in chusing the President, the Votes shall be taken by States, the Representation from each State having one Vote; a quorum for this Purpose shall consist of a Member or Members from two thirds of the States, and a Majority of all the States shall be necessary to a Choice. In every Case, after the Choice of the President, the Person having the greatest Number of Votes of the Electors shall be the Vice President. But if there should remain two or more who

have equal Votes, the Senate shall chuse from them by Ballot the Vice-President.]*

The Congress may determine the Time of chusing the Electors, and the Day on which they shall give their Votes; which Day shall be the same throughout the United States.

No person except a natural born Citizen, or a Citizen of the United States, at the time of the Adoption of this Constitution, shall be eligible to the Office of President; neither shall any Person be eligible to that Office who shall not have attained to the Age of thirty-five Years, and been fourteen Years a Resident within the United States.

**[In Case of the Removal of the President from Office, or of his Death, Resignation, or Inability to discharge the Powers and Duties of the said Office, the same shall devolve on the Vice President, and the Congress may by Law, provide for the Case of Removal, Death, Resignation or Inability, both of the President and Vice President, declaring what Officer shall then act as President, and such Officer shall act accordingly, until the Disability be removed, or a President shall be elected.]

The President shall, at stated Times, receive for his Services, a Compensation, which shall neither be encreased nor diminished during the Period for which he shall have been elected, and he shall not receive within that Period any other Emolument from the United States, or any of them.

Before he enter on the Execution of his Office, he shall take the following Oath or Affirmation:—"I do solemnly swear (or affirm) that I will faithfully execute the Office of President of the United States, and will to the best of my Ability, preserve, protect and defend the Constitution of the United States."

SECTION 2. The President shall be Commander in Chief of the Army and Navy of the United States, and of the Militia of the several States, when called into the actual Service of the United States; he may require the Opinion in writing, of the principal Officer in each of the executive Departments, upon any subject relating to the Duties of their respective Offices, and he shall have Power to Grant Reprieves and Pardons for Offenses against the United States, except in Cases of Impeachment.

He shall have Power, by and with the Advice and Consent of the Senate, to make Treaties, provided two-thirds of the Senators present concur; and he shall nominate, and by and with the Advice and Consent of the Senate, shall appoint Ambassadors, other public Ministers and Consuls, Judges of the supreme Court, and all other Officers of the United States, whose Appointments are not herein otherwise provided for, and which shall be established by Law: but the Congress may by Law vest the Appointment of such inferior Officers, as they think proper, in the President alone, in the Courts of Law, or in the Heads of Departments.

The President shall have Power to fill up all Vacancies that may happen during the Recess of the Senate, by granting Commissions which shall expire at the End of their next Session.

SECTION 3. He shall from time to time give to the Congress Information of the State of the Union, and recommend to their Consideration such Measures as he shall judge necessary and expedient; he may, on extraordinary Occasions, convene both Houses, or either of them, and in Case of Disagreement between them, with Respect to the Time of Adjournment, he may adjourn them to such Time as he shall think proper; he shall receive Ambassadors and other public

---

*Superseded by the twelfth amendment.

**This clause has been affected by the twenty-fifth amendment.

Ministers; he shall take Care that the Laws be faithfully executed, and shall Commission all the Officers of the United States.

SECTION 4. The President, Vice President and all civil Officers of the United States, shall be removed from Office on Impeachment for, and Conviction of, Treason, Bribery, or other high Crimes and Misdemeanors.

ARTICLE III.

SECTION I. The judicial Power of the United States, shall be vested in one supreme Court, and in such inferior Courts as the Congress may from time to time ordain and establish. The Judges, both of the supreme and inferior Courts, shall hold their Offices during good Behaviour, and shall, at stated Times, receive for their Services, a Compensation, which shall not be diminished during their Continuance in Office.

SECTION 2. The judicial Power shall extend to all Cases, in Law and Equity, arising under this Constitution, the Laws of the United States, and Treaties made, or which shall be made, under their Authority;—to all Cases affecting Ambassadors, other public Ministers and Consuls;—to all Cases of admiralty and maritime Jurisdiction;—to Controversies to which the United States shall be a Party;—to Controversies between two or more States;—between a State and Citizens of another State;—between Citizens of different States;—between Citizens of the same State claiming Lands under Grants of different States, and between a State, or the Citizens thereof, and foreign States, Citizens or Subjects.

In all Cases affecting Ambassadors, other public Ministers and Consuls, and those in which a State shall be Party, the supreme Court shall have original Jurisdiction. In all the other Cases before mentioned, the supreme Court shall have appellate Jurisdiction, both as to Law and Fact, with such Exceptions, and under such Regulations as the Congress shall make.

The trial of all Crimes, except in Cases of Impeachment, shall be by Jury; and such Trial shall be held in the State where the said Crimes shall have been committed; but when not committed within any State, the Trial shall be at such Place or Places as the Congress may by Law have directed.

SECTION 3. Treason against the United States, shall consist only in levying War against them, or in adhering to their Enemies, giving them Aid and Comfort. No Person shall be conficted of Treason unless on the Testimony of two Witnesses to the same overt Act, or on Confession in open Court.

The Congress shall have Power to declare the Punishment of Treason, but no Attainder of Treason shall work Corruption of Blood, or Forfeiture except during the Life of the Person attained.

ARTICLE IV.

SECTION I. Full Faith and Credit shall be given in each State to the public Acts, Records, and judicial Proceedings of every other State. And the Congress may by general Laws prescribe the Manner in which such Acts, Records and Proceedings shall be proved, and the Effect thereof.

SECTION 2. The Citizens of each State shall be entitled to all Privileges and Immunities of Citizens in the several States.

A Person charged in any State with Treason, Felony, or other Crime, who shall flee from Justice, and be found in another State, shall on demand of the executive Authority of the State from which he fled, be delivered up, to be removed to the State having Jurisdiction of the Crime.

[No Person held to Service or Labour in one State, under the Laws thereof, escaping into another, shall, in Consequence of any Law or Regulation therein, be discharged from such Service or Labour, but shall be delivered up on Claim of the Party to whom such Service or Labour may be due.]*

SECTION 3. New States may be admitted by the Congress into this Union; but no new State shall be formed or erected within the Jurisdiction of any other State; nor any State be formed by the Junction of two or more States, or parts of States, without the Consent of the Legislatures of the States concerned as well as of the Congress.

The Congress shall have Power to dispose of and make all needful Rules and Regulations respecting the Territory or other Property belonging to the United States; and nothing in this Constitution shall be so construed as to Prejudice any Claims of the United States, or of any particular State.

SECTION 4. The United States shall guarantee to every State in this Union a Republican Form of Government, and shall protect each of them against Invasion; and on Application of the Legislature, or of the Executive (when the Legislature cannot be convened) against domestic Violence.

ARTICLE V.

The Congress, whenever two-thirds of both Houses shall deem it necessary, shall propose Amendments to this Constitution, or, on the Application of the Legislatures of two-thirds of the several States, shall call a Convention for proposing Amendments, which, in either Case, shall be valid to all Intents and Purposes, as part of this Constitution, when ratified by the Legislatures of three-fourths of the several States, or by Conventions in three-fourths thereof, as the one or the other Mode of Ratification may be proposed by the Congress: Provided that no Amendment which may be made prior to the Year One thousand eight hundred and eight shall in any Manner affect the first and fourth Clauses in the Ninth Section of the first Article; and that no State, without its Consent, shall be deprived of its equal Suffrage in the Senate.

ARTICLE VI.

All Debts contracted and Engagements entered into, before the Adoption of this Constitution, shall be as valid against the United States under this Constitution, as under the Confederation.

This Constitution, and the Laws of the United States which shall be made in Pursuance thereof; and all Treaties made, or which shall be made, under the Authority of the United States, shall be the supreme Law of the Land; and the Judges in every State shall be bound thereby, any Thing in the Constitution or Laws of any State to the Contrary notwithstanding.

The Senators and Representatives before mentioned, and the Members of the several State Legislatures, and all executive and judicial Officers, both of the United States and of the several States, shall be bound by Oath or Affirmation, to support this Constitution; but no religious Test shall ever be required as a Qualification to any Office or public Trust under the United States.

---

*Superseded by the thirteenth amendment.

ARTICLE VII.

The Ratification of the Conventions of nine States shall be sufficient for the Establishment of this Constitution between the States so ratifying the Same.

DONE in Convention by the Unanimous Consent of the States present the Seventeenth Day of September in the Year of our Lord one thousand seven hundred and Eighty seven and of the Independence of the United States of America the Twelfth.

In Witness whereof We have hereunto subscribed our Names.

Go WASHINGTON
Presidt and deputy from Virginia

New Hampshire.
John Langdon
Nicholas Gilman

Connecticut.
Wm Saml Johnson
Roger Sherman

Massachusetts.
Nathaniel Gorham
Rufus King

New York.
Alexander Hamilton

New Jersey.
Wil: Livingston
David Brearley.
Wm Paterson.
Jona: Dayton

Maryland.
James McHenry
Danl Carrol
Dan: of St Thos Jenifer

Pennsylvania.
B Franklin
Robt. Morris
Thos. FitzSimons
James Wilson
Thomas Mifflin
Geo. Clymer
Jared Ingersoll
Gouv Morris

Virginia.
John Blair
James Madison Jr.

North Carolina.
Wm Blount
Hu Williamson
Richd Dobbs Spaight.

Delaware.
Geo: Read
John Dickinson
Jaco: Broom
Gunning Bedford jun
Richard Bassett

South Carolina.
J. Rutledge
Charles Pinckney
Charles Cotesworth Pinckney
Pierce Butler

Georgia.
William Few
Abr Baldwin

Attest:

WILLIAM JACKSON, *Secretary*

ARTICLES IN ADDITION TO, AND AMENDMENT OF, THE CONSTITUTION OF THE UNITED STATES OF AMERICA, PROPOSED BY CONGRESS, AND RATIFIED BY THE LEGISLATURES OF THE SEVERAL STATES, PURSUANT TO THE FIFTH ARTICLE OF THE ORIGINAL CONSTITUTION.*

(The first 10 Amendments were ratified December 15, 1791, and form what is known as the "Bill of Rights")

AMENDMENT I

Congress shall make no law respecting an establishment of religion, or prohibiting the free exercise thereof; or abridging the freedom of speech, or of the press; or the right of the people peaceably to assemble, and to petition the Government for a redress of grievances.

AMENDMENT II

A well regulated Militia, being necessary to the security of a free State, the right of the people to keep and bear Arms, shall not be infringed.

AMENDMENT III

No Soldier shall, in time of peace be quartered in any house, without the consent of the Owner, nor in time of war, but in a manner to be prescribed by law.

AMENDMENT IV

The right of the people to be secure in their persons, houses, papers, and effects, against unreasonable searches and seizures, shall not be violated, and no Warrants shall issue, but upon probable cause, supported by Oath or affirmation, and particularly describing the place to be searched, and the persons or things to be seized.

AMENDMENT V

No person shall be held to answer for a capital, or otherwise infamous crime, unless on a presentment or indictment of a Grand Jury, except in cases arising in the land or naval forces, or in the Militia, when in actual service in time of War or public danger; nor shall any person be subject for the same offence to be twice put in jeopardy of life or limb; nor shall be compelled in any criminal case to be a witness against himself, nor be deprived of life, liberty, or property, without due process of law; nor shall private property be taken for public use, without just compensation.

AMENDMENT VI

In all criminal prosecutions, the accused shall enjoy the right to a speedy and public trial, by an impartial jury of the State and district wherein the crime shall

---

*Amendment XXI was not ratified by state legislatures, but by state conventions summoned by Congress.

have been committed, which district shall have been previously ascertained by law, and to be informed of the nature and cause of the accusation; to be confronted with the witnesses against him; to have compulsory process for obtaining witnesses in his favor, and to have the Assistance of Counsel for his defence.

AMENDMENT VII

In suits at common law, where the value in controversy shall exceed twenty dollars, the right of trial by jury shall be preserved, and no fact tried by a jury, shall be otherwise reexamined in any Court of the United States, than according to the rules of the common law.

AMENDMENT VIII

Excessive bail shall not be required, nor excessive fines imposed, nor cruel and unusual punishments inflicted.

AMENDMENT IX

The enumeration in the Constitution, of certain rights, shall not be construed to deny or disparage others retained by the people.

AMENDMENT X

The powers not delegated to the United States by the Constitution, nor prohibited by it to the States, are reserved to the States respectively, or to the people.

AMENDMENT XI

(Ratified February 7, 1795)

The Judicial power of the United States shall not be construed to extend to any suit in law or equity, commenced or prosecuted against one of the United States by Citizens of another State, or by Citizens or Subjects of any Foreign State.

AMENDMENT XII

(Ratified June 15, 1804)

The Electors shall meet in their respective states and vote by ballot for President and Vice-President, one of whom, at least, shall not be an inhabitant of the same state with themseles; they shall name in their ballots the person voted for as President, and in distinct ballots the person voted for as Vice-President, and they shall make distinct lists of all persons voted for as President, and of all persons voted for as Vice-President, and of the number of votes for each, which lists they shall sign and certify, and transmit sealed to the seat of the government of the United States, directed to the President of the Senate;—The President of the Senate shall, in presence of the Senate and House of Representatives, open all the certificates and the votes shall then be counted;—The person having the greatest number of votes for President, shall be the President, if such number be

a majority of the whole number of Electors appointed; and if no person have such majority, then from the persons having the highest numbers not exceeding three on the list of those voted for as President, the House of Representatives shall choose immediately, by ballot, the President. But in choosing the President, the votes shall be taken by states, the representation from each state having one vote; a quorum for this purpose shall consist of a member or members from two-thirds of the states, and a majority of all the states shall be necessary to a choice. [And if the House of Representatives shall not choose a President whenever the right of choice shall devolve upon them, before the fourth day of March next following, then the Vice-President shall act as President, as in the case of the death or other constitutional disability of the President.—]* The person having the greatest number of votes as Vice-President, shall be the Vice-President, if such number be a majority of the whole number of Electors appointed, and if no person have a majority, then from the two highest numbers on the list, the Senate shall choose the Vice-President; a quorum for the purpose shall consist of two-thirds of the whole number of Senators, and a majority of the whole number shall be necessary to a choice. But no person constitutionally ineligible to the office of President shall be eligible to that of Vice-President of the United States.

AMENDMENT XIII

(Ratified December 6, 1865)

SECTION 1. Neither slavery nor involuntary servitude, except as a punishment for crime whereof the party shall have been duly convicted, shall exist within the United States, or any place subject to their jurisdiction.

SECTION 2. Congress shall have power to enforce this article by appropriate legislation.

AMENDMENT XIV

(Ratified July 9, 1868)

SECTION 1. All persons born or naturalized in the United States, and subject to the jurisdiction thereof, are citizens of the United States and of the State wherein they reside. No State shall make or enforce any law which shall abridge the privileges or immunities of citizens of the United States; nor shall any State deprive any person of life, liberty, or property, without due process of law; nor deny to any person within its jurisdiction the equal protection of the laws.

SECTION 2. Representatives shall be apportioned among the several States according to their respective numbers, counting the whole number of persons in each State, excluding Indians not taxed. But when the right to vote at any election for the choice of electors for President and Vice-President of the United States, Representatives in Congress, the Executive and Judicial officers of a State, or the members of the Legislature thereof, is denied to any of the male inhabitants of such State, being twenty-one years of age,* and citizens of the United States, or in any way abridged, except for participation in rebellion, or other crime, the basis of representation therein shall be reduced in the proportion which the number of such male citizens shall bear to the whole number of male citizens

---

*Superseded by section 3 of the twentieth amendment.

*Changed by section 1 of the twenty-sixth amendment.

twenty-one years of age in such State.

SECTION 3. No person shall be a Senator or Representative in Congress, or elector of President and Vice-President, or hold any office, civil or military, under the United States, or under any State, who, having previously taken an oath, as a member of Congress, or as an officer of the United States, or as a member of any State, legislature, or as an executive or judicial officer of any State, to support the Constitution of the United States, shall have engaged in insurrection or rebellion against the same, or given aid or comfort to the enemies thereof. But Congress may by a vote of two-thirds of each House, remove such disability.

SECTION 4. The validity of the public debt of the United States, authorized by law, including debts incurred for payment of pensions and bounties for services in suppressing insurrection or rebellion, shall not be questioned. But neither the United States nor any State shall assume or pay any debt or obligation incurred in aid of insurrection or rebellion against the United States, or any claim for the loss or emancipation of any slave; but all such debts, obligations and claims shall be held illegal and void.

SECTION 5. The Congress shall have power to enforce, by appropriate legislation, the provisions of this article.

AMENDMENT XV

(Ratified February 3, 1870)

SECTION I. The right of citizens of the United States to vote shall not be denied or abridged by the United States or by any State on account of race, color, or previous condition of servitude—

SECTION 2. The Congress shall have power to enforce this article by appropriate legislation.

AMENDMENT XVI

(Ratified February 3, 1913)

The Congress shall have power to lay and collect taxes on incomes, from whatever source derived, without apportionment among the several States, and without regard to any census or enumeration.

AMENDMENT XVII

(Ratified April 8, 1913)

The Senate of the United States shall be composed of two Senators from each State, elected by the people thereof, for six years; and each Senator shall have one vote. The electors in each State shall have the qualifications requisite for electors of the most numerous branch of the State legislatures.

When vacancies happen in the representation of any State in the Senate, the executive authority of such State shall issue writs of election to fill such vacancies: *Provided*, That the legislature of any State may empower the executive thereof to make temporary appointments until the people fill the vacancies by election as the legislature may direct.

This amendment shall not be so construed as to affect the election or term of any Senator chosen before it becomes valid as part of the Constitution.

AMENDMENT XVIII

(Ratified January 16, 1919)

[SECTION 1. After one year from the ratification of this article the manufacture, sale, or transportation of intoxicating liquors within, the importation thereof into, or the exportation thereof from the United States and all territory subject to the jurisdiction thereof for beverage purposes is hereby prohibited.

[SECTION 2. The Congress and the several States shall have concurrent power to enforce this article by appropriate legislation.

[SECTION 3. This article shall be inoperative unless it shall have been ratified as an amendment to the Constitution by the legislatures of the several States as provided in the Constitution, within seven years from the date of the submission hereof to the States by the Congress.]*

AMENDMENT XIX

(Ratified August 18, 1920)

The right of citizens of the United States to vote shall not be denied or abridged by the United States or by any State on account of sex.

Congress shall have power to enforce this article by appropriate legislation.

AMENDMENT XX

(Ratified January 23, 1933)

SECTION 1. The terms of the President and Vice President shall end at noon on the 20th day of January, and the terms of Senators and Representatives at noon on the 3rd day of January, of the years in which such terms would have ended if this article had not been ratified; and the terms of their successors shall then begin.

SECTION 2. The Congress shall assemble at least once in every year, and such meeting shall begin at noon on the 3rd day of January, unless they shall by law appoint a different day.

SECTION 3. If, at the time fixed for the beginning of the term of the President, the President elect shall have died, the Vice President elect shall become President. If a President shall not have been chosen before the time fixed for the beginning of his term, or if the President elect shall have failed to qualify, then the Vice President elect shall act as President until President shall have qualified; and the Congress may by law provide for the case wherein neither a President elect nor a Vice President elect shall have qualified, declaring who shall then act as President, or the manner in which one who is to act shall be selected, and such person shall act accordingly until a President or Vice President shall have qualified.

SECTION 4. The Congress may by law provide for the case of the death of any of the persons from whom the House of Representatives may choose a President whenever the right of choice shall have devolved upon them, and for the case of the death of any of the persons from whom the Senate may choose a Vice President whenever the right of choice shall have devolved upon them.

SECTION 5. Sections 1 and 2 shall take effect on the 15th day of October

---

*Repealed by section 1 of the twenty-first amendment.

following the ratification of this article.

SECTION 6. This article shall be inoperative unless it shall have been ratified as an amendment to the Constitution by the legislatures of three-fourths of the several States within seven years from the date of its submission.

AMENDMENT XXI

(Ratified December 5, 1933)

SECTION 1. The eighteenth article of amendment to the Constitution of the United States is hereby repealed.

SECTION 2. The transportation or importation into any State, Territory, or possession of the United States for delivery or use therein of intoxicating liquors, in violation of the laws thereof, is hereby prohibited.

SECTION 3. This article shall be inoperative unless it shall have been ratified as an amendment to the Constitution by conventions in the several States, as provided in the Constitution, within seven years from the date of the submission hereof to the States by the Congress.

AMENDMENT XXII

(Ratified February 27, 1951)

SECTION 1. No person shall be elected to the office of the President more than twice, and no person who has held the office of President, or acted as President, for more than two years of a term to which some other person was elected President shall be elected to the office of the President more than once. But this Article shall not apply to any person holding the office of President when this Article was proposed by the Congress, and shall not prevent any person who may be holding the office of President, or acting as President, during the term within which this Article becomes operative from holding the office of President or acting as President during the remainder of such term.

SECTION 2. This article shall be inoperative unless it shall have been ratified as an amendment to the Constitution by the legislatures of three-fourths of the several States within seven years from the date of its submission to the States by the Congress.

AMENDMENT XXIII

(Ratified March 29, 1961)

SECTION 1. The District constituting the seat of Government of the United States shall appoint in such manner as the Congress may direct:

A number of electors of President and Vice President equal to the whole number of Senators and Representatives in Congress to which the District would be entitled if it were a State, but in no event more than the least populous State; they shall be in addition to those appointed by the States, but they shall be considered, for the purposes of the election of President and Vice President, to be electors appointed by a State; and they shall meet in the District and perform such duties as provided by the twelfth article of amendment.

SECTION 2. The Congress shall have power to enforce this article by appropriate legislation.

AMENDMENT XXIV

(Ratified January 23, 1964)

SECTION 1. The right of citizens of the United States to vote in any primary or other election for President or Vice President, for electors for President or Vice President, or for Senator or Representative in Congress, shall not be denied or abridged by the United States or any State by reason of failure to pay any poll tax or other tax.

SECTION 2. The Congress shall have power to enforce this article by appropriate legislation.

AMENDMENT XXV

(Ratified February 10, 1967)

SECTION 1. In case of the removal of the President from office or of his death or resignation, the Vice President shall become President.

SECTION 2. Whenever there is a vacancy in the office of the Vice President, the President shall nominate a Vice President who shall take office upon confirmation by a majority vote of both Houses of Congress.

SECTION 3. Whenever the President transmits to the President pro tempore of the Senate and the Speaker of the House of Representatives his written declaration that he is unable to discharge the powers and duties of his office, and until he transmits to them a written declaration to the contrary, such powers and duties shall be discharged by the Vice President as Acting President.

SECTION 4. Whenever the Vice President and a majority of either the principal officers of the executive departments or of such other body as Congress may by law provide, transmit to the President pro tempore of the Senate and the Speaker of the House of Representatives their written declaration that the President is unable to discharge the powers and duties of his office, the Vice President shall immediately assume the powers and duties of the office as Acting President.

Thereafter, when the President transmits to the President pro tempore of the Senate and the Speaker of the House of Representatives his written declaration that no inability exists, he shall resume the powers and duties of his office unless the Vice President and a majority of either the principal officers of the executive department or of such other body as Congress may by law provide, transmit within four days to the President pro tempore of the Senate and the Speaker of the House of Representatives their written declaration that the President is unable to discharge the powers and duties of his office. Thereupon Congress shall decide the issue, assembling within forty-eight hours for that purpose if not in session. If the Congress, within twenty-one days after receipt of the latter written declaration, or, if Congress is not in session, within twenty-one days after Congress is required to assemble, determines by two-thirds vote of both Houses that the President is unable to discharge the powers and duties of his office, the Vice President shall continue to discharge the same as Acting President; otherwise, the President shall resume the powers and duties of his office.

AMENDMENT XXVI

(Ratified July 1, 1971)

SECTION 1. The right of citizens of the United States, who are eighteen years

of age or older, to vote shall not be denied or abridged by the United States or by any State on account of age.

SECTION 2. The Congress shall have power to enforce this article by appropriate legislation.

———————————— O ————————————

NOTES

INDEX TO THE CONSTITUTION AND AMENDMENTS

	Article [1]	Section	Clause
A			
Abridged. The privileges or immunities of citizens of the United States shall not be. [Amendments]	14	1	
Absent members, in such manner and under such penalties as it may provide. Each House is authorized to compel the attendance of	1	5	1
Accounts of receipts and expenditures of public money shall be published from time to time. A statement of the	1	9	7
Accusation. In all criminal prosecutions the accused shall be informed of the cause and nature of the. [Amendments]	6		
Accused shall have a speedy public trial. In all criminal prosecutions the. [Amendments]	6		
He shall be tried by an impartial jury of the State and district where the crime was committed. [Amendments]	6		
He shall be informed of the nature of the accusation. [Amendments]	6		
He shall be confronted with the witnesses against him. [Amendments]	6		
He shall have compulsory process for obtaining witnesses in his favor. [Amendments]	6		
He shall have the assistance of counsel for his defense. [Amendments]	6		
Actions at common law involving over twenty dollars shall be tried by jury. [Amendments]	7*		
Acts, records, and judicial proceedings of another State. Full faith and credit shall be given in each State to the	4	1	
Acts. Congress shall prescribe the manner of proving such acts, records, and proceedings	4	1	
Adjourn from day to day. A smaller number than a quorum of each House may	1	5	1
Adjourn for more than three days, nor to any other place than that in which they shall be sitting. Neither House shall, during the session of Congress, without the consent of the other	1	5	4
Adjournment, the President may adjourn them to such time as he shall think proper. In case of disagreement between the two Houses as to	2	3	
Admiralty and maritime jurisdiction. The judicial power shall extend to all cases of	3	2	1
Admitted by the Congress into this Union, but no new States shall be formed or erected within the jurisdiction of any other State. New States may be	4	3	1
Nor shall any State be formed by the junction of two or more States, or parts of States, without the consent of the legislatures and of Congress	4	3	1
Adoption of the Constitution shall be valid. All debts and engagements contracted by the confederation and before the	6		1

[1] Article of original Constitution or of amendment.

27

	Article [1]	Section	Clause
Advice and consent of the Senate. The President shall have power to make treaties by and with the	2	2	2
To appoint ambassadors or other public ministers and consuls by and with the	2	2	2
To appoint all other officers of the United States not herein otherwise provided for by and with the	2	2	2
Affirmation. Senators sitting to try impeachments shall be on oath or	1	3	6
To be taken by the President of the United States. Form of the oath or	2	1	7
No warrants shall be issued but upon probable cause and on oath or. [Amendments]	4		
To support the Constitution. Senators and Representatives, members of State legislatures, executive and judicial officers, both State and Federal, shall be bound by oath or	6		3
Age. No person shall be a Representative who shall not have attained twenty-five years of	1	2	2
No person shall be a Senator who shall not have attained thirty years of	1	3	3
Right of citizens of the United States, who are eighteen years of age or older, to vote shall not be denied or abridged by the United States or any State on account of age. [Amendments]	26	1	
Agreement or compact with another State without the consent of Congress. No State shall enter into any	1	10	3
Aid and comfort. Treason against the United States shall consist in levying war against them, adhering to their enemies, and giving them	3	3	1
Alliance or confederation. No State shall enter into any treaty of	1	10	1
Ambassadors, or other public ministers and consuls. The President may appoint	2	2	2
The judicial power of the United States shall extend to all cases affecting	3	2	1
Amendments to the Constitution. Whenever two-thirds of both Houses shall deem it necessary, Congress shall propose	5		
On application of the legislatures of two-thirds of the States, Congress shall call a convention to propose	5		
Shall be valid when ratified by the legislatures of, or by conventions in, three-fourths of the States	5		
Answer for a capital or infamous crime unless on presentment of a grand jury. No person shall be held to. [Amendments]	5		
Except in cases in the land or naval forces, or in the militia when in actual service. [Amendments]	5		
Appellate jurisdiction both as to law and fact, with such exceptions and under such regulations as Congress shall make. In what cases the Supreme Court shall have	3	2	2
Application of the legislature or the executive of a State. The United States shall protect each State against invasion and domestic violence on the	4	4	
Application of the legislatures of two-thirds of the States, Congress shall call a convention for proposing amendments to the Constitution. On the	5		
Appointment of officers and authority to train the militia reserved to the States respectively	1	8	16
Of such inferior officers as they may think proper in the President alone. Congress may by law vest the	2	2	2
In the courts of law or in the heads of departments. Congress may by law vest the	2	2	2
Of Presidential and Vice-Presidential electors. District of Columbia to have power of. [Amendments]	23	1	

[1] Article of original Constitution or of amendment.

	Article [1]	Section	Clause
Apportionment of representation and direct taxation among the several States. Provisions relating to the___	1	2	3
Congress shall have power to lay and collect taxes on incomes, from whatever source derived, without apportionment among the several States_____	16	_____	_____
Of Representatives among the several States. Provisions relating to the. [Amendments]_____	14	2	_____
Appropriate legislation. Congress shall have power to make all laws necessary and proper for carrying into execution the foregoing powers, and all other powers vested by the Constitution in the Government of the United States, or in any department or officer thereof_	1	8	18
Congress shall have power to enforce the thirteenth article, prohibiting slavery by. [Amendments]____	13	2	_____
Congress shall have power to enforce the provisions of the fourteenth article by. [Amendments]_____	14	5	_____
Congress shall have power to enforce the provisions of the fifteenth article by. [Amendment]_____	15	2	_____
Congress shall have power to enforce the provisions of the twenty-third article by. [Amendments]____	23	2	_____
Congress shall have power to enforce the provisions of the twenty-fourth article by. [Amendments]_____	24	2	_____
Congress shall have power to enforce the provisions of the twenty-sixth article by. [Amendments]_____	26	2	_____
Appropriation of money for raising and supporting armies shall be for a longer term than two years. But no_____	1	8	12
Appropriations made by law. No money shall be drawn from the Treasury but in consequence of_____	1	9	7
Approve and sign a bill before it shall become a law. The President shall_____	1	7	2
He shall return it to the House in which it originated, with his objections, if he does not_____	1	7	2
Armies, but no appropriation for that use shall be for a longer term than two years. Congress shall have power to raise and support_____	1	8	12
Armies. Congress shall make rules for the government and regulation of the land and naval forces_____	1	8	14
Arms shall not be infringed. A well-regulated militia being necessary to the security of a free State, the right of the people to keep and bear. [Amendments]_____	2	_____	_____
Arrest during their attendance at the session of their respective Houses, and in going to and returning from the same. Members shall in all cases, except treason, felony, and breach of the peace, be privileged from_____	1	6	1
Arsenals. Congress shall exercise exclusive authority over all places purchased for the erection of_____	1	8	17
Articles exported from any State. No tax or duty shall be laid on_____	1	9	5
Arts by securing to authors and inventors their patent rights. Congress may promote the progress of science and the useful_____	1	8	8
Assistance of counsel for his defense. In all criminal prosecutions the accused shall have the. [Amendments]_____	6	_____	_____
Assumption of the debt or obligations incurred in aid of rebellion or insurrection against the United States. Provisions against the. [Amendments]_____	14	4	_____
Attainder or ex post facto law shall be passed. No bill of__	1	9	3
Attainder, ex post facto law, or law impairing the obligation of contracts. No State shall pass any bill of_____	1	10	1
Attainder of treason shall not work corruption of blood or forfeiture, except during the life of the person attainted__	3	3	2
Authors and inventors the exclusive right to their writings and inventions. Congress shall have power to secure to_	1	8	8

[1] Article of original Constitution or of amendment.

	Article [1]	Section	Clause

B

Bail. Excessive bail shall not be required, nor excessive fines nor cruel and unusual punishments imposed. [Amendments]_____

	Article [1]	Section	Clause
Bail. Excessive bail shall not be required, nor excessive fines nor cruel and unusual punishments imposed. [Amendments]	8		
Ballot for President and Vice President. The electors shall vote by. [Amendment]	12		
Ballot. If no person have a majority of the electoral votes for President and Vice President, the House of Representatives shall immediately choose the President by. [Amendments]	12		
Bankruptcies. Congress shall have power to pass uniform laws on the subject of	1	8	4
Basis of representation among the several States. Provisions relating to the. [Amendments]	14	2	
Bear arms shall not be infringed. A well-regulated militia being necessary to the security of a free State, the right of the people to keep and. [Amendments]	2		
Behavior. The judges of the Supreme and inferior courts shall hold their offices during good	3	1	
Bill of attainder or ex post facto law shall be passed. No	1	9	3
Bill of attainder, ex post facto law, or law impairing the obligation of contracts. No State shall pass any	1	10	1
Bills of credit. No State shall emit	1	10	1
Bills for raising revenue shall originate in the House of Representatives. All	1	7	1
Bills which shall have passed the Senate and House of Representatives shall, before they become laws, be presented to the President	1	7	2
If he approve, he shall sign them; if he disapprove, he shall return them, with his objections, to that House in which they originated	1	7	2
Upon the reconsideration of a bill returned by the President with his objections, if two-thirds of each House agree to pass the same, it shall become a law	1	7	2
Upon the reconsideration of a bill returned by the President, the question shall be taken by yeas and nays	1	7	2
Not returned by the President within ten days (Sundays excepted), shall, unless Congress adjourn, become laws	1	7	2
Borrow money on the credit of the United States. Congress shall have power to	1	8	2
Bounties and pensions, shall not be questioned. The validity of the public debt incurred in suppressing insurrection and rebellion against the United States, including the debt for. [Amendments]	14	4	
Breach of the peace, shall be privileged from arrest while attending the session, and in going to and returning from the same. Senators and Representatives, except for treason, felony, and	1	6	1
Bribery, or other high crimes and misdemeanors. The President, Vice President, and all civil officers shall be removed on impeachment for and conviction of treason	2	4	

C

	Article [1]	Section	Clause
Capital or otherwise infamous crime, unless on indictment of a grand jury, except in certain specified cases. No person shall be held to answer for a. [Amendments]	5		
Capitation or other direct tax shall be laid unless in proportion to the census or enumeration. No	1	9	4

[1] Article of original Constitution or of amendment.

	Article [1]	Section	Clause
Captures on land and water. Congress shall make rules concerning_____	1	8	11
Casting vote. The Vice President shall have no vote unless the Senate be equally divided_____	1	3	4
Census or enumeration of the inhabitants shall be made within three years after the first meeting of Congress, and within every subsequent term of ten years thereafter_____	1	2	3
No capitation or other direct tax shall be laid except in proportion to the_____	1	9	4
Chief Justice shall preside when the President of the United States is tried upon impeachment. The_____	1	3	6
Choosing the electors and the day on which they shall give their votes, which shall be the same throughout the United States. Congress may determine the time of _____	2	1	3
Citizen of the United States at the adoption of the Constitution shall be eligible to the office of President. No person not a natural-born_____	2	1	4
Citizen of the United States. No person shall be a Senator who shall not have attained the age of thirty years, and been nine years a_____	1	3	3
No person shall be a Representative who shall not have attained the age of twenty-five years, and been seven years a_____	1	2	2
Right to vote shall not be denied or abridged by the United States or any State for failure to pay any poll tax or other tax. [Amendments]_____	24	1	_____
Right of citizens to vote shall not be denied or abridged by the United States or any State on account of sex. [Amendments]_____	19	_____	_____
Right to vote shall not be denied or abridged by the United States or any State to any citizen eighteen years or older, on account of age. [Amendments]___	26	1	_____
Citizenship. Citizens of each State shall be entitled to all the privileges and immunities of citizens of the several States_____	4	2	1
All persons born or naturalized in the United States, and subject to the jurisdiction thereof, are citizens of the United States and of the State in which they reside. [Amendments]_____	14	1	_____
No State shall make or enforce any law which shall abridge the privileges or immunities of citizens of the United States. [Amendments]_____	14	1	_____
Nor shall any State deprive any person of life, liberty, or property without due process of law. [Amendments]_____	14	1	_____
Nor deny to any person within its jurisdiction the equal protection of the laws. [Amendments]_____	14	1	_____
Citizens or subjects of a foreign state. The judicial power of the United States shall not extend to suits in law or equity brought against one of the States by the citizens of another State, or by. [Amendments]_____	11	_____	_____
Civil officers of the United States shall, on impeachment for and conviction of treason, bribery, and other high crimes and misdemeanors be removed. All_____	2	4	_____
Claims of the United States or any particular State in the territory or public property. Nothing in this Constitution shall be construed to prejudice_____	4	3	2

[1] Article of original Constitution or of amendment.

31

	Article [1]	Section	Clause
Classification of Senators. Immediately after they shall be assembled after the first election, they shall be divided as equally as may be into three classes	1	3	2
Classification of Senators. The seats of the Senators of the first class shall be vacated at the expiration of the second year	1	3	2
The seats of the Senators of the second class at the expiration of the fourth year	1	3	2
The seats of the Senators of the third class at the expiration of the sixth year.	1	3	2
Coin a tender in payment of debts. No State shall make anything but gold and silver	1	10	1
Coin money and regulate the value thereof and of foreign coin. Congress shall have power to	1	8	5
Coin of the United States. Congress shall provide for punishing the counterfeiting the securities and current.	1	8	6
Color, or previous condition of servitude. The right of citizens of the United States to vote shall not be denied or abridged by the United States or by any State on account of race. [Amendments]	15	1	------
Comfort. Treason against the United States shall consist in levying war against them, and giving their enemies aid and	3	3	1
Commander in chief of the Army and Navy, and of the militia when in actual service. The President shall be.	2	2	1
Commerce with foreign nations, among the States, and with Indian tribes. Congress shall have power to regulate	1	8	3
Commerce or revenue. No preference shall be given to the ports of one State over those of another by any regulation of	1	9	6
Vessels clearing from the ports of one State shall not pay duties in those of another	1	9	6
Commissions to expire at the end of the next session. The President may fill vacancies that happen in the recess of the Senate by granting	2	2	3
Common defense, promote the general welfare, &c. To insure the. [Preamble]	------	------	------
Common defense and general welfare. Congress shall have power to provide for the	1	8	1
Common law, where the amount involved exceeds twenty dollars, shall be tried by jury. Suits at. [Amendments]	7	------	------
No fact tried by a jury shall be otherwise reexamined in any court of the United States than according to the rules of the. [Amendments]	7	------	------
Compact with another State. No State shall, without consent of Congress, enter into any agreement or	1	10	3
Compact with a foreign power. No State shall, without the consent of Congress, enter into any agreement or	1	10	3
Compensation of Senators and Representatives to be ascertained by law	1	6	1
Compensation of the President shall not be increased nor diminished during the period for which he shall be elected.	2	1	6
Compensation of the judges of the Supreme and inferior courts shall not be diminished during their continuance in office	3	1	------
Compensation. Private property shall not be taken for public use without just. [Amendments]	5	------	------
Compulsory process for obtaining witnesses in his favor. In criminal prosecutions the accused shall have. [Amendments]	6	------	------

[1] Article of original Constitution or of amendment.

	Article [1]	Section	Clause
Confederation. No State shall enter into any treaty, alliance, or	1	10	1
Confederation. All debts contracted and engagements entered into before the adoption of this Constitution shall be valid against the United States under it, as under the	6	------	1
Confession in open court. Conviction of treason shall be on the testimony of two persons to the overt act, or upon	3	3	1
Congress of the United States. All legislative powers shall be vested in a	1	1	------
Shall consist of a Senate and House of Representatives	1	1	------
Shall assemble at least once in every year, which shall be on the first Monday of December, unless they by law appoint a different day	1	4	2
May at any time alter regulations for elections of Senators and Representatives, except as to the places of choosing Senators	1	4	1
Each House shall be the judge of the elections, returns, and qualifications of its own members	1	5	1
A majority of each House shall constitute a quorum to do business	1	5	1
A smaller number may adjourn from day to day and compel the attendance of absent members	1	5	1
Each House may determine the rules of its proceedings, punish its members for disorderly behavior, and, with the concurrence of two-thirds, expel a member	1	5	2
Each House shall keep a journal of its proceedings	1	5	3
Neither House, during the session of Congress, shall, without the consent of the other, adjourn for more than three days	1	5	4
Senators and Representatives shall receive a compensation to be ascertained by law	1	6	1
They shall in all cases, except treason, felony, and breach of peace, be privileged from arrest during attendance at their respective Houses, and in going to and returning from the same	1	6	1
No Senator or Representative shall, during his term, be appointed to any civil office which shall have been created, or of which the emoluments shall have been increased, during such term	1	6	2
No person holding any office under the United States, shall, while in office, be a member of either House of Congress	1	6	2
All bills for raising revenue shall originate in the House of Representatives	1	7	1
Proceedings in cases of bills returned by the President with his objections	1	7	2
Shall have power to lay and collect duties, imposts, and excises, pay the debts, and provide for the common defense and general welfare	1	8	1
Shall have power to borrow money on the credit of the United States	1	8	2
To regulate foreign and domestic commerce, and with the Indian tribes	1	8	3
To establish uniform rule of naturalization and uniform laws on the subject of bankruptcies	1	8	4
To coin money, regulate its value and the value of foreign coin, and to fix the standard of weights and measures	1	8	5
To punish the counterfeiting of securities and current coin of the United States	1	8	6

[1] Article of original Constitution or of amendment.

	Article [1]	Section	Clause
Congress of the United States—Continued			
To establish post-offices and post-roads	1	8	7
To promote the progress of science and the useful arts	1	8	8
To constitute tribunals inferior to the Supreme Court	1	8	9
To define and punish piracies and felonies on the high seas and to punish offenses against the law of nations	1	8	10
To declare war, grant letters of marque and reprisal, and make rules concerning captures on land and water	1	8	11
To raise and support armies, but no appropriations of money to that use shall be for a longer term than two years	1	8	12
To provide and maintain a Navy	1	8	13
To make rules for the government of the Army and Navy	1	8	14
To call out the militia to execute the laws, suppress insurrections, and repel invasions	1	8	15
To provide for organizing, arming, and equipping the militia	1	8	16
To exercise exclusive legislation over the District fixed for the seat of government, and over forts, magazines, arsenals, and dockyards	1	8	17
To make all laws necessary and proper to carry into execution all powers vested by the Constitution in the Government of the United States	1	8	18
No person holding any office under the United States shall accept of any present, emolument, office or title of any kind from any foreign state, without the consent of	1	9	8
May determine the time of choosing the electors for President and Vice-President and the day on which they shall give their votes	2	1	3
The President may, on extraordinary occasions, convene either House of	2	3	
The manner in which the acts, records, and judicial proceedings of the States shall be prescribed by	4	1	
New States may be admitted by Congress into this Union	4	3	1
Shall have power to make all needful rules and regulations respecting the territory or other property belonging to the United States	4	3	2
Amendments to the Constitution shall be proposed whenever it shall be deemed necessary by two-thirds of both Houses of	5		
Persons engaged in insurrection or rebellion against the United States disqualified for Senators or Representatives in. [Amendments]	14	3	
But such disqualification may be removed by a vote of two-thirds of both Houses of. [Amendments]	14	3	
Shall have power to enforce, by appropriate legislation, the thirteenth amendment. [Amendments]	13	2	
Shall have power to enforce, by appropriate legislation, the fourteenth amendment. [Amendments]	14	5	
Shall have power to enforce, by appropriate legislation, the fifteenth amendment. [Amendments]	15	2	
Shall have power to enforce, by appropriate legislation, the nineteenth amendment. [Amendments]	19		
Sessions, time of assembling. [Amendments]	20	2	
Shall have power to enforce, by appropriate legislation, the twenty-third amendment. [Amendments]	23	2	

[1] Article of original Constitution or of amendment.

	Article [1]	Section	Clause
Congress of the United States—Continued			
Shall have power to enforce, by appropriate legislation, the twenty-fourth amendment. [Amendments]	24	2	------
Shall have power to enforce, by appropriate legislation, the twenty-sixth amendment. [Amendments]	26	2	------
To direct appointment of electors for President and Vice-President by District of Columbia. [Amendments]	23	1	------
Consent. No State shall be deprived of its equal suffrage in the Senate without its	5	------	------
Consent of Congress. No person holding any office of profit or trust under the United States shall accept of any present, emolument, office, or title of any kind whatever, from any king, prince, or foreign potentate, without the	1	9	8
No State shall lay any imposts, or duties on imports, except what may be absolutely necessary for executing its inspection laws, without the	1	10	2
No State shall lay any duty of tonnage, keep troops or ships of war in time of peace, without the	1	10	3
No State shall enter into any agreement or compact with another State, or with a foreign power, without the	1	10	3
No State shall engage in war unless actually invaded, or in such imminent danger as will not admit of delay, without the	1	10	3
No new State shall be formed or erected within the jursidiction of any other State, nor any State be formed by the junction of two or more States, or parts of States, without the consent of the legislatures thereof, as well as the	4	3	1
Consent of the legislature of the State in which the same may be. Congress shall exercise exclusive authority over all places purchased for the erection of forts, magazines, arsenals, dockyards, and other needful buildings by the	1	8	17
Consent of the legislatures of the States and of Congress. No States shall be formed by the junction of two or more States or parts of States without the	4	3	1
Consent of the other. Neither House, during the session of Congress, shall adjourn for more than three days, nor to any other place than that in which they shall be sitting, without the	1	5	4
Consent of the owner. No soldier shall be quartered in time of peace in any house without the. [Amendments]	3	------	------
Consent of the Senate. The President shall have power to make treaties, by and with the advice and	2	2	2
The President shall appoint ambassadors, other public ministers and consuls, judges of the Supreme Court and all other officers created by law and not otherwise herein provided for, by and with the advice and	2	2	2
Constitution, in the Government of the United States, or in any department or officer thereof. Congress shall have power to pass all laws necessary to the execution of the powers vested by the	1	8	18
Constitution, shall be eligible to the office of President. No person except a natural-born citizen, or a citizen at the time of the adoption of the	2	1	4

[1] Article of original Constitution or of amendment.

	Article [1]	Section	Clause
Constitution. The President, before he enters upon the execution of his office, shall take an oath to preserve, protect, and defend the___	2	1	7
Constitution, laws, and treaties of the United States. The judicial power shall extend to all cases arising under the_	3	2	1
Constitution shall be so construed as to prejudice any claims of the United States, or of any State (in respect to territory or other property of the United States). Nothing in the___	4	3	2
Constitution. The manner in which amendments may be proposed and ratified___	5	------	------
Constitution. as under the Confederation shall be valid. All debts and engagements contracted before the adoption of the___	6	------	1
Constitution and the laws made in pursuance thereof, and all treaties made, or which shall be made, by the United States, shall be the supreme law of the land. The___	6	------	2
The judges in every State, anything in the constitution or laws of a State to the contrary notwithstanding, shall be bound thereby___	6	------	2
Constitution. All officers, legislative, executive, and judicial, of the United States, and of the several States, shall be bound by an oath to support the___	6	------	3
But no religious test shall ever be required as a qualification for any office or public trust___	6	------	3
Constitution between the States so ratifying the same. The ratification of the conventions of nine States shall be sufficient for the establishment of the___	7	------	------
Constitution, of certain rights, shall not be construed to deny or disparage others retained by the people. The enumeration in the. [Amendments]___	9	------	------
Constitution, nor prohibited by it to the States, are reserved to the States respectively or to the people. Powers not delegated to the United States by the. [Amendments]___	10	------	------
Constitution, and then engaged in rebellion against the United States. Disqualification for office imposed upon certain class of persons who took an oath to support the. [Amendments]___	14	3	------
Constitution. Done in convention by the unanimous consent of the States present, September 17, 1787___	7	------	2
Contracts. No State shall pass any ex post facto law, or law impairing the obligation of___	1	10	1
Controversies to which the United States shall be a party: between two or more States; between a State and citizens of another State; between citizens of different States; between citizens of the same State claiming lands under grants of different States; between a State or its citizens and foreign states, citizens, or subjects. The judicial power shall extend to___	3	2	1
Convene Congress or either House, on extraordinary occasions. The President may___	2	3	------
Convention for proposing amendments to the Constitution. Congress, on the application of two-thirds of the legislatures of the States, may call a___	5	------	------
Convention, by the unanimous consent of the States present on the 17th of September, 1787. Adoption of the Constitution in___	7	------	2
Conventions of nine States shall be sufficient for the establishment of the Constitution. The ratification of the___	7	------	------

[1] Article of original Constitution or of amendment.

36

	Article [1]	Section	Clause
Conviction in cases of impeachment shall not be had without the concurrence of two-thirds of the members present	1	3	6
Copyrights to authors for limited times. Congress shall have power to provide for	1	8	8
Corruption of blood. Attainder of treason shall not work	3	3	2
Counsel for his defense. In all criminal prosecutions the accused shall have the assistance of. [Amendments]	6		
Counterfeiting the securities and current coin of the United States. Congress shall provide for the punishment of	1	8	6
Courts. Congress shall have power to constitute tribunals inferior to the Supreme Court	1	8	9
Courts of law. Congress may by law vest the appointment of such inferior officers as they think proper in the President alone, in the heads of departments, or in the	2	2	2
Courts as Congress may establish. The judicial power of the United States shall be vested in one Supreme Court and such inferior	3	1	
Courts. The judges of the Supreme and inferior courts shall hold their offices during good behavior	3	1	
Their compensation shall not be diminished during their continuance in office	3	1	
Credit. No State shall emit bills of	1	10	1
Credit of the United States. Congress shall have power to borrow money on the	1	8	2
Credit shall be given in every other State to the public acts, records, and judicial proceedings of each State. Full faith and	4	1	
Crime, unless on a presentment of a grand jury. No person shall be held to answer for a capital or otherwise infamous. [Amendments]	5		
Except in cases in the military and naval forces, or in the militia when in actual service. [Amendments]	5		
Crimes and misdemeanors. The President, Vice President, and all civil officers shall be removed on impeachment for and conviction of treason, bribery, or other	2	4	
Crimes, except in cases of impeachment, shall be tried by jury. All	3	2	3
They shall be tried in the State within which they may be committed	3	2	3
When not committed in a State, they shall be tried at the places which Congress may by law have provided	3	2	3
Criminal prosecutions, the accused shall have a speedy and public trial by jury in the State and district where the crime was committed. In all. [Amendments]	6		
He shall be informed of the nature and cause of the accusation. [Amendments]	6		
He shall be confronted with the witnesses against him. [Amendments]	6		
He shall have compulsory process for obtaining witnesses in his favor. [Amendments]	6		
He shall have the assistance of counsel in his defense. [Amendments]	6		
Criminate himself. No person as a witness shall be compelled to. [Amendments]	5		
Cruel and unusual punishments inflicted. Excessive bail shall not be required, nor excessive fines imposed, nor. [Amendments]	8		

[1] Article of original Constitution or of amendment.

	Article [1]	Section	Clause

D

	Article [1]	Section	Clause
Danger as will not admit of delay. No State shall, without the consent of Congress, engage in war, unless actually invaded, or in such imminent	1	10	3
Day on which they shall vote for President and Vice President, which shall be the same throughout the United States. Congress may determine the time of choosing the electors, and the	2	1	3
Day to day, and may be authorized to compel the attendance of absent members. A smaller number than a quorum of each House may adjourn from	1	5	1
Death, resignation, or inability of the President, the powers and duties of his office shall devolve on the Vice President. In case of the	2	1	5
[Amendments]	25		
Death, resignation, or inability of the President. Congress may provide by law for the case of the removal	2	1	5
[Amendments]	25		
Debt of the United States, including debts for pensions and bounties incurred in suppressing insurrection or rebellion, shall not be questioned. The validity of the public. [Amendments]	14	4	
Debts. No State shall make anything but gold and silver coin a tender in payment of	1	10	1
Debts and provide for the common defense and general welfare of the United States. Congress shall have power to pay the	1	8	1
Debts and engagements contracted before the adoption of this Constitution shall be as valid against the United States, under it, as under the Confederation	6		1
Debts or obligations incurred in aid of insurrection or rebellion against the United States, or claims for the loss or emancipation of any slave. Neither the United States nor any State shall assume or pay any. [Amendments]	14	4	
Declare war, grant letters of marque and reprisal, and make rules concerning captures on land and water. Congress shall have power to	1	8	11
Defense, promote the general welfare, &c. To insure the common. [Preamble]			
Defense and general welfare throughout the United States. Congress shall have power to pay the debts and provide for the common	1	8	1
Defense. In all criminal prosecutions the accused shall have the assistance of counsel for his. [Amendments]	6		
Delaware entitled to one Representative in the First Congress	1	2	3
Delay. No State shall, without the consent of Congress, engage in war unless actually invaded, or in such imminent danger as will not admit of	1	10	3
Delegated to the United States, nor prohibited to the States, are reserved to the States or to the people. The powers not. [Amendments]	10		
Deny of disparage others retained by the people. The enumeration in the Constitution of certain rights shall not be construed to. [Amendments]	9		
Departments upon any subject relating to their duties. The President may require the written opinion of the principal officers in each of the executive	2	2	1

[1] Article of original Constitution or of amendment.

	Article [1]	Section	Clause
Departments. Congress may by law vest the appointment of inferior officers in the heads of	2	2	2
Direct tax shall be laid unless in proportion to the census or enumeration. No capitation or other	1	9	4
Direct taxes and Representatives, how apportioned among the several States	1	2	3
Disability of the President and Vice President. Provisions in case of the	2	1	5
[Amendments]	25		
Disability. No person shall be a Senator or Representative in Congress, or presidential elector, or hold any office, civil or military, under the United States, or any State, who having previously taken an oath as a legislative, executive, or judicial officer of the United States, or of any State, to support the Constitution, afterward engaged in insurrection or rebellion against the United States. [Amendments]	14	3	
But Congress may, by a vote of two-thirds of each House, remove such. [Amendments]	14	3	
Disagreement between the two Houses as to the time of adjournment, the President may adjourn them to such time as he may think proper. In case of	2	3	
Disorderly behavior. Each House may punish its members for	1	5	2
And with the concurrence of two-thirds expel a member	1	5	2
Disparage others retained by the people. The enumeration in the Constitution of certain rights shall not be construed to deny or. [Amendments]	9		
Disqualification. No Senator or Representative shall, during the time for which he was elected, be appointed to any office under the United States which shall have been created or its emoluments increased during such term	1	6	2
No person holding any office under the United States shall be a member of either House during his continuance in office	1	6	2
No person shall be a member of either House, presidential elector, or hold any office under the United States, or any State, who, having previously sworn to support the Constitution, afterward engaged in insurrection or rebellion. [Amendments]	14	3	
Disqualification. But Congress may, by a vote of two-thirds of each House, remove such disability. [Amendments]	14	3	
District of Columbia. Congress shall exercise exclusive legislation in all cases over the	1	8	17
Electors for President and Vice-President, appointment by. [Amendments]	23	1	
Dockyards. Congress shall have exclusive authority over all places purchased for the erection of	1	8	17
Domestic tranquility, provide for the common defense, &c. To insure. [Preamble]			
Domestic violence. The United States shall protect each State against invasion and	4	4	
Due process of law. No person shall be compelled, in any criminal case, to be a witness against himself, nor be deprived of life, liberty, or property without. [Amendments]	5		
No State shall deprive any person of life, liberty, or property without. [Amendments]	14	1	

[1] Article of original Constitution or of amendment.

	Article [1]	Section	Clause
Duties and powers of the office of President, in case of his death, removal or inability to act, shall devolve on the Vice President	2	1	5
[Amendments]	25		
In case of the disability of the President and Vice President, Congress shall declare what officer shall act	2	1	5
[Amendments]	25		
Duties, imposts, and excise. Congress shall have power to lay and collect taxes	1	8	1
Shall be uniform throughout the United States	1	8	1
Duties shall be laid on articles exported from any State. No tax or	1	9	5
Duties in another State. Vessels clearing in the ports of one State shall not be obliged to pay	1	9	6
On imports and exports, without the consent of Congress, except where necessary for executing its inspection laws. No State shall lay any	1	10	2
The net produce of all such duties shall be for the use of the Treasury of the United States	1	10	2
All laws laying such duties shall be subject to the revision and control of Congress	1	10	2
Duty of tonnage without the consent of Congress. No State shall lay any	1	10	3

E

Eighteenth Amendment. Repeal. [Amendments]	21	1	
Election of President and Vice President. Congress may determine the day for the	2	1	3
Shall be the same throughout the United States. The day of the	2	1	3
Elections. The right of citizens of the United States to vote in shall not be denied or abridged by the United States or any State by reason of failure to pay any poll tax or other tax. [Amendments]	24	1	
Elections for Senator and Representatives. The legislatures of the States shall prescribe the times, places, and manner of holding	1	4	1
But Congress may, at any time, alter such regulations, except as to the places of choosing Senators	1	4	1
Returns and qualifications of its own members. Each House shall be the judge of the	1	5	1
Senators elected by the people. [Amendments]	17	1	
Electors for members of the House of Representatives. Qualifications of	1	2	1
Electors for Senators. Qualifications of. [Amendments]	17	1	
Electors for President and Vice President. Each State shall appoint, in such manner as the legislature thereof may direct, a number of electors equal to the whole number of Senators and Representatives to which the State may be entitled in the Congress	2	1	2
But no Senator or Representative, or person holding an office of trust or profit under the United States, shall be appointed an elector	2	1	2
Congress may determine the time of choosing the electors and the day on which they shall give their votes	2	1	3
Which day shall be the same throughout the United States	2	1	3

[1] Article of original Constitution or of amendment.

	Article [1]	Section	Clause
Electors for President and Vice President—Continued			
The electors shall meet in their respective States and vote by ballot for President and Vice President, one of whom, at least, shall not be an inhabitant of the same State with themselves. [Amendments]	12		
District of Columbia to appoint, in such manner as the Congress may direct, a number of electors equal to the whole number of Senators and Representatives to which the District would be entitled if it were a State. [Amendments]	23	1	
Electors shall name, in their ballots, the person voted for as President; and in distinct ballots the person voted for as Vice President. [Amendments]	12		
They shall make distinct lists of the persons voted for as President and of persons voted for as Vice President, which they shall sign and certify, and transmit sealed to the seat of government, directed to the President of the Senate. [Amendments]	12		
No person having taken an oath as a legislative, executive or judicial officer of the United States, or of any State, and afterwards engaged in insurrection or rebellion against the United States, shall be an elector	14	3	
But Congress may, by a vote of two-thirds of each House remove such disability. [Amendments]	14	3	
Emancipation of any slave shall be held to be illegal and void. Claims for the loss or. [Amendments]	14	4	
Emit bills of credit. No State shall	1	10	1
Emolument of any kind from any king, prince, or foreign state, without the consent of Congress. No person holding any office under the United States shall accept any	1	9	8
Enemies. Treason shall consist in levying war against the United States, in adhering to, or giving aid and comfort to their	3	3	1
Engagements contracted before the adoption of this Constitution shall be valid. All debts and	6		1
Enumeration of the inhabitants shall be made within three years after the first meeting of Congress, and within every subsequent term of ten years thereafter	1	2	3
Ratio of representation not to exceed one for every 30,000 until the first enumeration shall be made	1	2	3
Income tax authorized without regard to. [Amendments]	16		
Enumeration in the Constitution of certain rights shall not be construed to deny or disparage others retained by the people. The. [Amendments]	9		
Equal protection of the laws. No State shall deny to any person within its jurisdiction the. [Amendments]	14	1	
Equal suffrage in the Senate. No State shall be deprived without its consent, of its	5		
Establishment of this Constitution between the States ratifying the same. The ratification of nine States shall be sufficient for the	7		
Excessive bail shall not be required, nor excessive fines imposed, nor cruel and unusual punishments inflicted. [Amendments]	8		
Excises. Congress shall have power to lay and collect taxes, duties, imposts, and	1	8	1
Shall be uniform throughout the United States. All duties, imposts, and	1	8	1

[1] Article of original Constitution or of amendment.

	Article [1]	Section	Clause
Exclusive legislation, in all cases, over such district as may become the seat of government. Congress shall exercise_	1	8	17
Over all places purchased for the erection of forts, magazines, arsenals, dock-yards, and other needful buildings. Congress shall exercise_____	1	8	17
Executive of a State. The United States shall protect each State against invasion and domestic violence, on the application of the legislature or the_____	4	4	_____
Executive and judicial officers of the United States and of the several States shall be bound by an oath to support the Constitution_____	6	_____	3
Executive departments. On subjects relating to their duties the President may require the written opinions of the principal officers in each of the_____	2	2	1
Congress may by law vest the appointment of inferior officers in the heads of_____	2	2	2
Executive power shall by vested in a President of the United States of America. The_____	2	1	1
Expel a member. Each House, with the concurrence of two-thirds, may_____	1	5	2
Expenditures of public money shall be published from time to time. A regular statement of the receipts and_____	1	9	7
Exportations from any State. No tax or duty shall be laid on_____	1	9	5
Exports or imports, except upon certain conditions. No State shall, without the consent of Congress, lay any duties on_____	1	10	2
Laid by any State, shall be for the use of the Treasury. The net produce of all duties on_____	1	10	2
Shall be subject to the revision and control of Congress. All laws of the States laying duties on_____	1	10	2
Ex post facto law shall be passed. No bill of attainder or_	1	9	3
Ex post facto law, or law impairing the obligation of contracts. No State shall pass any bill of attainder_____	1	10	1
Extraordinary occasions. The President may convene both houses, or either House of Congress, on_____	2	3	_____

F

Faith and credit in each State shall be given to the acts, records, and judicial proceedings of another State. Full_	4	1	_____
Felony, and breach of the peace. Members of Congress shall not be privileged from arrest for treason_____	1	6	1
Felonies committed on the high seas. Congress shall have power to define and punish piracies and_____	1	8	10
Fines. Excessive fines shall not be imposed. [Amendments]_____	8	_____	_____
Foreign coin. Congress shall have power to coin money, fix the standard of weights and measures, and to regulate the value of_____	1	8	5
Foreign nations, among the States, and with the Indian tribes. Congress shall have power to regulate commerce with_____	1	8	3
Foreign power. No State shall, without the consent of Congress, enter into any compact or agreement with any_____	1	10	3
Forfeiture, except during the life of the person attainted. Attainder of treason shall not work_____	3	3	2
Formation of new States. Provisions relating to the_____	4	3	1

[1] Article of original Constitution or of amendment.

	Article [1]	Section	Clause
Form of government. The United States shall guarantee to every State in this Union a republican_____	4	4	_____
And shall protect each of them against invasion; and on application of the legislature or of the executive (when the legislature cannot be convened), against domestic violence_____	4	4	_____
Forts, magazines, arsenals, dock-yards, and other needful buildings. Congress shall exercise exclusive authority over all places purchased for the erection of_____	1	8	17
Freedom of speech or of the press. Congress shall make no law abridging the. [Amendments]_____	1	_____	_____
Free State, the right of the people to keep and bear arms shall not be infringed. A well-regulated militia being necessary to the security of a. [Amendments]_____	2	_____	_____
Fugitives from crime found in another State shall, on demand, be delivered up to the authorities of the State from which they may flee_____	4	2	2
Fugitives from service or labor in one State, escaping into another State, shall be delivered up to the party to whom such service or labor may be due_____	4	2	3

G

General welfare and secure the blessings of liberty, &c. To promote the. [Preamble]_____	_____	_____	_____
General welfare. Congress shall have power to provide for the common defense and_____	1	8	1
Georgia shall be entitled to three Representatives in the first Congress_____	1	2	3
Gold and silver coin a tender in payment of debts. No State shall make anything but_____	1	10	1
Good behavior. The judges of the Supreme and inferior courts shall hold their offices during_____	3	1	_____
Government. The United States shall guarantee to every State in this Union a republican form of_____	4	4	_____
And shall protect each of them against invasion, and on application of the legislature or of the executive (when the legislature cannot be convened), against domestic violence_____	4	4	_____
Grand jury. No person shall be held to answer for a capital or otherwise infamous crime, unless on the presentment of a. [Amendments]_____	5	_____	_____
Except in cases arising in the land and naval forces, and in the militia when in actual service. [Amendments]_____	5	_____	_____
Guarantee to every State in this Union a republican form of government. The United States shall_____	4	4	_____
And shall protect each of them against invasion; and on application of the legislature or of the executive (when the legislature cannot be convened), against domestic violence_____	4	4	_____

H

Habeas corpus shall not be suspended unless in cases of rebellion or invasion. The writ of_____	1	9	2
Heads of departments. Congress may, by law, vest the appointment of inferior officers in the_____	2	2	2
On any subject relating to their duties, the President may require the written opinion of the principal officer in each of the executive departments_____	2	2	1

[1] Article of original Constitution or of amendment.

Index to the Constitution—Continued

	Article [1]	Section	Clause
High crimes and misdemeanors. The President, Vice President, and all civil officers shall be removed on impeachment for and conviction of treason, bribery, or other	2	4	------
House of Representatives. Congress shall consist of a Senate and	1	1	------
Shall be composed of members chosen every second year	1	2	1
Qualifications of electors for members of the	1	2	1
No person shall be a member who shall not have attained the age of twenty-five years, and been seven years a citizen of the United States	1	2	2
The executives of the several States shall issue writs of election to fill vacancies in the	1	2	4
Shall choose their Speaker and other officers	1	2	5
Shall have the sole power of impeachment	1	2	5
Shall be the judge of the elections, returns, and qualifications of its own members	1	5	1
A majority shall constitute a quorum to do business	1	5	1
Less than a majority may adjourn from day to day, and compel the attendance of absent members	1	5	1
May determine its own rules of proceedings	1	5	2
May punish its members for disorderly behavior, and, with the concurrence of two-thirds, expel a member	1	5	2
Shall keep a journal of its proceedings	1	5	3
Shall not adjourn for more than three days during the session of Congress without the consent of the Senate	1	5	4
Members shall not be questioned for any speech or debate in either House or in any other place	1	6	1
No person holding any office under the United States shall, while holding such office, be a member, of the	1	6	2
No person, while a member of either House, shall be appointed to an office which shall have been created or the emoluments increased during his membership	1	6	2
All bills for raising revenue shall originate in the	1	7	1
The votes for President and Vice President shall be counted in the presence of the Senate and. [Amendments]	12	------	------
If no person have a majority of electoral votes, then from the three highest on the list the House of Representatives shall immediately, by ballot, choose a President. [Amendments]	12	------	------
They shall vote by States, each State counting one vote. [Amendments]	12	------	------
A quorum shall consist of a member or members from two-thirds of the States, and a majority of all the States shall be necessary to the choice of a President. [Amendments]	12	------	------
No person having as a legislative, executive, or judicial officer of the United States, or of any State, taken an oath to support the Constitution, and afterwards engaged in insurrection or rebellion against the United States, shall be a member of the. [Amendments]	14	3	------
But Congress may, by a vote of two-thirds of each House, remove such disability. [Amendments]	14	3	------

[1] Article of original Constitution or of amendment.

44

	Article [1]	Section	Clause
I			
Imminent danger as will not admit of delay. No State shall, without the consent of Congress, engage in war, unless actually invaded or in such	1	10	3
Immunities. Members of Congress shall, in all cases except treason, felony, and breach of the peace, be privileged from arrest during their attendance at the session of their respective houses, and in going and returning from the same	1	6	1
No soldier shall be quartered in any house without the consent of the owner in time of peace. [Amendments]	3	------	------
Immunities. No person shall be twice put in jeopardy of life and limb for the same offense. [Amendments]	5	------	------
All persons born or naturalized in the United States, and subject to the jurisdiction thereof, are citizens of the United States and of the State in which they reside. [Amendments]	14	1	------
No State shall make or enforce any law which shall abridge the privileges or immunities ot citizens of the United States. [Amendments]	14	1	------
Nor shall any State deprive any person of life, liberty, or property without due process of law. [Amendments]	14	1	------
Nor deny to any person within its jurisdiction the equal protection of the law. [Amendments]	14	1	------
Impeachment. The President may grant reprieves and pardons except in cases of	2	2	1
The House of Representatives shall have the sole power of	1	2	5
Impeachment for and conviction of treason, bribery, and other high crimes and misdemeanors. The President, Vice-President, and all civil officers shall be removed upon	2	4	------
Impeachments. The Senate shall have the sole power to try all	1	3	6
The Senate shall be on oath, or affirmation, when sitting for the trial of	1	3	6
When the President of the United States is tried the Chief Justice shall preside	1	3	6
No person shall be convicted without the concurrence of two-thirds of the members present	1	3	6
Judgment shall not extend beyond removal from office and disqualification to hold office	1	3	7
But the party convicted shall be liable to indictment and punishment according to law	1	3	7
Importation of slaves prior to 1808 shall not be prohibited by the Congress	1	9	1
But a tax or duty of ten dollars for each person may be imposed on such	1	9	1
Imports or exports except what may be absolutely necessary for executing its inspection laws. No State shall, without the consent of Congress, lay any imposts or duties on	1	10	2
Imports or exports laid by any State shall be for the use of the Treasury. The net produce of all duties on	1	10	2
Imports or exports shall be subject to the revision and control of Congress. All laws of States laying duties on	1	10	2

[1] Article of original Constitution or oi amendment.

	Article [1]	Section	Clause
Imposts and excises. Congress shall have power to lay and collect taxes, duties	1	8	1
Shall be uniform throughout the United States. All taxes, duties	1	8	1
Inability of the President, the powers and duties of his office shall devolve on the Vice President. In case of the death, resignation, or	2	1	5
[Amendments]	25		
Inability of the President or Vice President. Congress may provide by law for the case of the removal, death, resignation, or	2	1	5
[Amendments]	25		
Income taxes. Congress shall have power to lay and collect without apportionment among the several States, and without regard to any census or enumeration. [Amendments]	16		
Indian tribes. Congress shall have power to regulate commerce with the	1	8	3
Indictment or presentment of a grand jury. No person shall be held to answer for a capital or infamous crime unless on. [Amendments]	5		
Except in cases arising in the land and naval forces, and in the militia when in actual service. [Amendments]	5		
Indictment, trial, judgment, and punishment, according to law. The party convicted in case of impeachment shall nevertheless be liable and subject to	1	3	7
Infamous crime unless on presentment or indictment of a grand jury. No person shall be held to answer for a capital or. [Amendments]	5		
Inferior courts. Congress shall have power to constitute tribunals inferior to the Supreme Court	1	8	9
Inferior courts as Congress may establish. The judicial power of the United States shall be vested in one Supreme Court and such	3	1	
The judges of both the Supreme and inferior courts shall hold their offices during good behavior	3	1	
Their compensation shall not be diminished during their continuance in office	3	1	
Inferior officers in the courts of law, in the President alone, or in the heads of Departments. Congress, if they think proper, may by law vest the appointment of	2	2	2
Inhabitant of the State for which he shall be chosen. No person shall be a Senator who shall not have attained the age of thirty years, been nine years a citizen of the United States, and who shall not, when elected, be an	1	3	3
Insurrection or rebellion against the United States. No person shall be a Senator or Representative in Congress, or presidential elector, or hold any office, civil or military, under the United States, or any State, who having taken an oath as a legislative, executive, or judicial officer of the United States, or of a State, afterwards engaged in. [Amendments]	14	3	
But Congress may, by a vote of two-thirds of each House, remove such disabilities. [Amendments]	14	3	
Debts declared illegal and void which were contracted in aid of. [Amendments]	14	4	
Insurrections and repel invasions. Congress shall provide for calling forth the militia to suppress	1	8	15

[1] Article of original Constitution or of amendment.

	Article[1]	Section	Clause
Intoxicating liquors. Prohibition of manufacture, sale, transportation, importation or exportation of. [Amendments]	18	1	------
Repeal of Eighteenth Amendment. [Amendments]	21	1	------
Transportation or importation into any State, Territory or possession, for delivery or use therein, in violation of their laws, prohibited. [Amendments]	21	2	------
Invasion. No State shall, without the consent of Congress engage in war unless actually invaded, or in such imminent danger as will not admit of delay	1	10	3
Invasion. The writ of habeas corpus shall not be suspended unless in case of rebellion or	1	9	2
Invasion and domestic violence. The United States shall protect each State against	4	4	------
Invasions. Congress shall provide for calling forth the militia to suppress insurrections and repel	1	8	15
Inventors and authors in their inventions and writings. Congress may pass laws to secure for limited times exclusive rights to	1	8	8
Involuntary servitude, except as a punishment for crime, abolished in the United States. Slavery and. [Amendments]	13	1	------

J

	Article[1]	Section	Clause
Jeopardy of life and limb for the same offense. No person shall be twice put in. [Amendments]	5	------	------
Journal of its proceedings. Each House shall keep a	1	5	3
Judges in every State shall be bound by the Constitution, the laws and treaties of the United States, which shall be the supreme law of the land	6	------	2
Judges of the Supreme and inferior courts shall hold their offices during good behavior	3	1	------
Their compensation shall not be diminished during their continuance in office	3	1	------
Judgment in cases of impeachment shall not extend further than to removal from office, and disqualification to hold any office of honor, trust, or profit under the United States	1	3	7
But the party convicted shall nevertheless be liable and subject to indictment, trial, judgment, and punishment according to law	1	3	7
Judicial power of the United States. Congress shall have power to constitute tribunals inferior to the Supreme Court	1	8	9
The judicial power of the United States shall be vested in one Supreme Court, and in such inferior courts as Congress may from time to time ordain and establish	3	1	------
The judges of the Supreme and inferior courts shall hold their offices during good behavior	3	1	------
Their compensation shall not be diminished during their continuance in office	3	1	------
It shall extend to all cases in law and equity arising under the Constitution, laws, and treaties of the United States	3	2	1
To all cases affecting ambassadors, other public ministers, and consuls	3	2	1
To all cases of admiralty and maritime jurisdiction	3	2	1
To controversies to which the United States shall be a party	3	2	1
To controversies between two or more States	3	2	1
To controversies between a State and citizens of another State	3	2	[2] 1

[1] Article of original Constitution or of amendment.
[2] See also the eleventh amendment.

	Article [1]	Section	Clause
Judicial power of the United States—Continued			
To controversies between citizens of different States	3	2	1
To citizens of the same State claiming lands under grants of different States	3	2	1
To controversies between a State or its citizens and foreign states, citizens, or subjects	3	2	1
In all cases affecting ambassadors, other public ministers and consuls, and those in which a State shall be a party, the Supreme Court shall have original jurisdiction	3	2	2
In all other cases before mentioned, it shall have appellate jurisdiction, both as to law and fact, with such exceptions and under such regulations as Congress shall make	3	2	2
The trial of all crimes, except in cases of impeachment, shall be by jury	3	2	3
The trial shall be held in the State where the crimes shall have been committed	3	2	3
But when not committed in a State, the trial shall be at such place or places as Congress may by law have directed	3	2	3
The judicial power of the United States shall not be held to extend to any suit in law or equity commenced or prosecuted against one of the United States by citizens of another State, or by citizens or subjects of any foreign State. [Amendments]	11	------	------
Judicial proceedings of every other State. Full faith and credit shall be given in each State to the acts, records, and	4	1	------
Congress shall prescribe the manner of proving such acts, records, and proceedings	4	1	------
Judicial and executive officers of the United States and of the several States shall be bound by an oath to support the Constitution	6	------	3
Judiciary. The Supreme Court shall have original jurisdiction in all cases affecting ambassadors, other public ministers and consuls, and those in which a State may be a party	3	2	2
The Supreme Court shall have appellate jurisdiction both as to law and fact, with such exceptions and regulations as Congress may make	3	2	2
Junction of two or more States or parts of States without the consent of the legislatures and of Congress. No State shall be formed by the	4	3	1
Jurisdiction of another State. No new State shall, without the consent of Congress, be formed or erected within the	4	3	1
Jurisdiction, both as to law and fact, with such exceptions and under such regulations as Congress may make. The Supreme Court shall have appellate	3	2	2
Jurisdiction. In all cases affecting ambassadors and other public ministers and consuls, and in cases where a State is a party, the Supreme Court shall have original	3	2	2
Jury. The trial of all crimes, except in cases of impeachment, shall be by	3	2	3
In all criminal prosecutions the accused shall have a speedy and public trial by. [Amendments]	6	------	------
All suits at common law, where the value exceeds twenty dollars, shall be tried by. [Amendments]	7	------	------
Where a fact has been tried by a jury it shall not be reexamined except by the rules of the common law. [Amendments]	7	------	------

[1] Article of original Constitution or of amendment.

48

	Article [1]	Section	Clause
Just compensation. Private property shall not be taken for public use without. [Amendments]	5		
Justice, insure domestic tranquility, &c. To establish. [Preamble]			

L

	Article [1]	Section	Clause
Labor, in one State escaping into another State shall be delivered up to the party to whom such service or labor may be due. Fugitives from service or	4	2	3
Land and naval forces. Congress shall make rules for the government and regulation of the	1	8	14
Law and fact, with exceptions and under regulations to be made by Congress. The Supreme Court shall have appellate jurisdiction as to	3	2	2
Law of the land. The Constitution, the laws made in pursuance thereof, and treaties of the United States, shall be the supreme	6		2
The Judges in every State shall be bound thereby	6		2
Law of nations. Congress shall provide for punishing offenses against the	1	8	10
Laws. Congress shall provide for calling forth the militia to supress insurrection, repel invasion, and to execute the	1	8	15
Laws and treaties of the United States. The judicial power shall extend to all cases in law and equity arising under the Constitution, or the	3	2	1
Laws necessary to carry into execution the powers vested in the government, or in any department or officer of the United States. Congress shall make all	1	8	18
Legal tender in payment of debts. No State shall make anything but gold and silver coin a	1	10	1
Legislation in all cases over such district as may become the seat of government. Congress shall exercise exclusive	1	8	17
Over all places purchased for the erection of forts, magazines, arsenals, dock-yards, and other needful buildings. Congress shall exercise exclusive	1	8	17
Legislation. Congress shall have power to make all laws necessary and proper for carrying into execution all the powers vested by the Constitution in the Government of the United States or in any department or officer thereof	1	8	18
Legislation. Congress shall have power to enforce article xiii, prohibiting slavery, by appropriate. [Amendments]	13	2	
Congress shall have power to enforce the fourteenth amendment by appropriate. [Amendments]	14	5	
Congress shall have power to enforce the fifteenth amendment by appropriate. [Amendments]	15	2	
Legislative powers herein granted shall be vested in Congress. All	1	1	
Legislature, or the Executive (when the legislature cannot be convened). The United States shall protect each State against invasion and domestic violence, on the application of the	4	4	
Legislatures of two-thirds of the States, Congress shall call a convention for proposing amendments to the Constitution. On the application of the	5		
Letters of marque and reprisal. Congress shall have power to grant	1	8	11
No State shall grant	1	10	1

[1] Article of original Constitution or of amendment.

	Article [1]	Section	Clause
Liberty to ourselves and our posterity, &c. To secure the blessings of. [Preamble]_____			
Life, liberty, and property without due process of law. No person shall be compelled in any criminal case to be a witness against himself, nor be deprived of. [Amendments]_____	5		
No State shall abridge the privileges or immunities of citizens of the United States, nor deprive any person of. [Amendments]_____	14	1	
Life or limb for the same offense. No person shall be twice put in jeopardy of. [Amendments]_____	5		
Loss or emancipation of any slave shall be held illegal and void. Claims for the. [Amendments]_____	14	4	

M

	Article [1]	Section	Clause
Magazines, arsenals, dock-yards, and other needful buildings. Congress shall have exclusive authority over all places purchased for the erection of_____	1	8	17
Majority of each House shall consititute a quorum to do business. A_____	1	5	1
But a smaller number may adjourn from day to day and may be authorized to compel the attendance of absent members_____	1	5	1
Majority of all the States shall be necessary to a choice. When the choice of a President shall devolve on the House of Representatives, a quorum shall consist of a member or members from two-thirds of the States; but a. [Amendments]_____	12		
When the choice of a Vice President shall devolve on the Senate, a quorum shall consist of two-thirds of the whole number of Senators, and a majority of the whole number shall be necessary to a choice. [Amendments]_____	12		
Maritime jurisdiction. The judicial power shall extend to all cases of admiralty and_____	3	2	1
Marque and reprisal. Congress shall have power to grant letters of_____	1	8	11
No State shall grant any letters of_____	1	10	1
Maryland entitled to six Representatives in the first Congress_____	1	2	3
Massachusetts entitled to eight Representatives in the first Congress_____	1	2	3
Measures. Congress shall fix the standard of weights and_	1	8	5
Meeting of Congress. The Congress shall assemble at least once in every year, and such meeting shall be on the first Monday in December, unless they shall by law appoint a different day_____	1	4	2
Meeting of electors. District of Columbia, electors for President and Vice-President appointed by District. [Amendments]_____	23	1	
Members of Congress and of State legislatures shall be bound by oath or affirmation to support the Constitution_____	6		3
Militia to execute the laws, suppress insurrections, and repel invasions. Congress shall provide for calling forth the_____	1	8	15
Congress shall provide for organizing, arming, and disciplining the_____	1	8	16

[1] Article of original Constitution or of amendment.

	Article [1]	Section	Clause
Militia to execute the laws, suppress insurrections, and repel invasions. Congress shall provide for governing such part of them as may be employed by the United States	1	8	16
Reserving to the States the appointment of the officers and the right to train the militia according to the discipline prescribed by Congress	1	8	16
A well-regulated militia being necessary to the security of a free State, the right of the people to keep and bear arms shall not be infringed. [Amendments]	2		
Misdemeanors. The President, Vice President, and all civil officers shall be removed on impeachment for and conviction of treason, bribery, or other high crimes and	2	4	
Money on the credit of the United States. Congress shall have the power to borrow	1	8	2
Regulate the value thereof and of foreign coin. Congress shall have power to coin	1	8	5
Shall be drawn from the Treasury but in consequence of appropriations made by law. No	1	9	7
Shall be published from time to time. A regular statement and account of receipts and expenditures of public	1	9	7
For raising and supporting armies. No appropriation of money shall be for a longer term than two years	1	8	12

N

	Article [1]	Section	Clause
Nations. Congress shall have power to regulate commerce with foreign	1	8	3
Congress shall provide for punishing offenses against the law of	1	8	10
Natural-born citizen, or a citizen at the adoption of the Constitution, shall be eligible to the office of President. No person except a	2	1	4
Naturalization. Congress shall have power to establish a uniform rule of	1	8	4
Naturalized in the United States, and subject to their jurisdiction, shall be citizens of the United States and of the States in which they reside. All persons born, or. [Amendments]	14	1	
Naval forces. Congress shall make rules and regulations for the government and regulation of the land and	1	8	14
Navy. Congress shall have power to provide and maintain a	1	8	13
New Hampshire entitled to three Representatives in the first Congress	1	2	3
New Jersey entitled to four Representatives in the first Congress	1	2	3
New States may be admitted by Congress into this Union	4	3	1
But no new State shall be formed within the jurisdiction of another State without the consent of Congress	4	3	1
Nor shall any State be formed by the junction of two or more States or parts of States, without the consent of the legislatures and of Congress	4	3	1
New York entitled to six Representatives in the first Congress	1	2	3
Nobility shall be granted by the United States. No title of	1	9	8
No State shall grant any title of	1	10	1

[1] Article of original Constitution or of amendment.

	Article [1]	Section	Clause
Nominations for office by the President. The President shall nominate, and, by and with the advice and consent of the Senate, shall appoint ambassadors and other public officers	2	2	2
He may grant commissions to fill vacancies that happen in the recess of the Senate, which shall expire at the end of their next session	2	2	3
North Carolina entitled to five Representatives in the first Congress	1	2	3
Number of electors for President and Vice-President in each State shall be equal to the number of Senators and Representatives to which such State may be entitled in Congress	2	1	2

O

	Article [1]	Section	Clause
Oath of office of the President of the United States. Form of the	2	1	7
Oath or affirmation. No warrants shall be issued but upon probable cause supported by. [Amendments]	4		
Oath or affirmation to support the Constitution. Senators and Representatives, members of State legislatures, executive and judicial officers of the United States and of the several States, shall be bound by	6		3
But no religious test shall ever be required as a qualification for office	6		3
The Senators when sitting to try impeachment shall be on	1	3	6
Objections. If he shall not approve it, the President shall return the bill to the House in which it originated with his	1	7	2
Obligation of contracts. No State shall pass any ex post facto law, or law impairing the	1	10	1
Obligations incurred in aid of insurrection or rebellion against the United States to be held illegal and void. All debts or. [Amendments]	14	4	
Offense. No person shall be twice put in jeopardy of life or limb for the same. [Amendments]	5		
Offenses against the law of nations. Congress shall provide for punishing	1	8	10
Against the United States, except in cases of impeachment. The President may grant reprieves or pardons for	2	2	1
Office under the United States. No person shall be a member of either House while holding any civil	1	6	2
No Senator or Representative shall be appointed to any office under the United States which shall have been created, or its emoluments increased, during the term for which he is elected	1	6	2
Or title of any kind from any king, prince, or foreign State, without the consent of Congress. No person holding any office under the United States shall accept of any present, emolument	1	9	8
Office of President, in case of his removal, death, resignation, or inability, shall devolve on the Vice President. The powers and duties of the	2	1	5
[Amendments]	25		
During the term of four years. The President and Vice President shall hold	2	1	1

[1] Article of original Constitution or of amendment.

52

	Article [1]	Section	Clause
Office of President—Continued			
Of trust or profit under the United States shall be an elector for President and Vice President. No person holding an_____	2	1	2
Civil or military under the United States, or any State, who had taken an oath as a legislative, executive, or judicial officer of the United States, or of any State, and afterward engaged in insurrection or rebellion. No person shall be a Senator, Representative, or Presidential elector, or hold any. [Amendments]_____	14	3	------
Officers in the President alone, in the courts of law, or in the heads of Departments. Congress may vest the appointment of Inferior_____	2	2	2
Of the United States shall be removed on impeachment for and conviction of treason, bribery, or other high crimes and misdemeanors. The President, Vice President, and all civil_____	2	4	------
The House of Representatives shall choose their Speaker and other_____	1	2	5
The Senate, in the absence of the Vice President, shall choose a President pro tempore, and also their other_____	1	3	5
Offices becoming vacant in the recess of the Senate may be filled by the President, the commissions to expire at the end of the next session_____	2	2	3
One-fifth of the members present, be entered on the journal of each House. The yeas and nays shall, at the desire of__	1	5	3
Opinion of the principal officers in each of the Executive Departments on any subject relating to their duties. The President may require the written_____	2	2	1
Order, resolution, or vote (except on a question of adjournment) requiring the concurrence of the two Houses, shall be presented to the President. Every_____	1	7	3
Original jurisdiction, in all cases affecting ambassadors, other public ministers, and consuls, and in which a State may be a party. The Supreme Court shall have_____	3	2	2
Overt act, or on confession in open court. Conviction of treason shall be on the testimony of two witnesses to the__	3	3	1
P			
Pardons, except in cases of impeachment. The President may grant reprieves and_____	2	2	1
Patent rights to inventors. Congress may pass laws for securing_____	1	8	8
Peace. Members of Congress shall not be privileged from arrest for treason, felony, and breach of the_____	1	6	1
No State shall, without the consent of Congress, keep troops or ships of war in time of_____	1	10	3
No soldier shall be quartered in any house without the consent of the owner in time of. [Amendments]___	3	------	------
Pensions and bounties shall not be questioned. The validity of the public debt incurred in suppressing insurrection and rebellion against the United States, including the debt for. [Amendments]_____	14	4	------
Pennsylvania entitled to eight Representatives in the first Congress_____	1	2	3

[1] Article of original Constitution or of amendment.

	Article [1]	Section	Clause
People, peaceably to assemble and petition for redress of grievances, shall not be abridged by Congress. The right of the. [Amendments]_____	1	------	------
To keep and bear arms shall not be infringed. A well-regulated militia being necessary to the security of a free State, the right of the. [Amendments]_____	2	------	------
To be secure in their persons, houses, papers, and effects, against unreasonable searches and seizures shall not be violated. The right of the. [Amendments]_____	4	------	------
People. The enumeration of certain rights in the Constitution shall not be held to deny or disparage others retained by the. [Amendments]_____	9	------	------
People. Powers not delegated to the United States, or prohibited to the States, are reserved to the States or to the. [Amendments]_____	10	------	------
Perfect Union, &c. To establish a more. [Preamble]____	------	------	------
Persons, houses, papers, and effects against unreasonable searches and seizures. The people shall be secure in their. [Amendments]_____	4	------	------
Persons, as any State may think proper to admit, shall not be prohibited prior to 1808. The migration or importation of such_____	1	9	1
But a tax or duty of ten dollars shall be imposed on the importation of each of such_____	1	9	1
Petition for the redress of grievances. Congress shall make no law abridging the right of the people peaceably to assemble and to. [Amendments]_____	1	------	------
Piracies and felonies committed on the high seas. Congress shall define and punish_____	1	8	10
Place than that in which the two Houses shall be sitting. Neither House during the session shall, without the consent of the other, adjourn for more than three days, nor to any other_____	1	5	4
Places of choosing Senators. Congress may by law make or alter regulations for the election of Senators and Representatives, except as to the_____	1	4	1
Poll tax. The right of citizens of the United States to vote shall not be denied or abridged by the United States or any State by reason of failure to pay. [Amendments]__	24	1	------
Ports of one State over those of another. Preference shall not be given by any regulation of commerce or revenue to the_____	1	9	6
Vessels clearing from the ports of one State shall not pay duties in another_____	1	9	6
Post offices and post roads. Congress shall establish_____	1	8	7
Powers herein granted shall be vested in Congress. All legislative_____	1	1	------
Powers vested by the Constitution in the Government or in any Department or officer of the United States. Congress shall make all laws necessary to carry into execution the_____	1	8	18
Powers and duties of the office shall devolve on the Vice President, on the removal, death, resignation, or inability of the President. The_____	2	1	5
[Amendments]_____ _____	25	------	------

[1] Article of original Constitution or of amendment.

	Article [1]	Section	Clause
Powers not delegated to the United States nor prohibited to the States are reserved to the States and to the people. [Amendments]	10	------	------
The enumeration of certain rights in this Constitution shall not be held to deny or disparage others retained by the people. [Amendments]	9	------	------
Preference, by any regulation of commerce or revenue, shall not be given to the ports of one State over those of another	1	9	6
Prejudice any claims of the United States or of any particular State in the territory or property of the United States. Nothing in this Constitution shall	4	3	2
Present, emolument, office, or title of any kind whatever from any king, prince, or foreign State. No person holding any office under the United States shall, without the consent of Congress, accept any	1	9	8
Presentment or indictment of a grand jury, except in cases arising in the land or naval forces, or in the militia when in actual service. No person shall be held to answer for a capital or otherwise infamous crime unless on a. [Amendments]	5	------	------
President of the United States. The Senate shall choose a President pro tempore when the Vice President shall exercise the office of	1	3	5
Additional provision for succession through act of Congress. [Amendments]	20	4	------
Succession in case of death. [Amendments]	20	3	------
Succession in case of failure to be chosen or qualified. [Amendments]	20	3	------
Term of office, beginning and ending. [Amendments]	20	1	------
The Chief Justice shall preside upon the trial of the	1	3	6
Shall approve and sign all bills passed by Congress before they shall become laws	1	7	2
Shall return to the House in which it originated, with his objections, any bill which he shall not approve	1	7	2
If not returned within ten days (Sundays excepted), it shall become a law, unless Congress shall adjourn before the expiration of that time	1	7	2
Every order, resolution, or vote which requires the concurrence of both Houses, except on a question of adjournment, shall be presented to the	1	7	3
If disapproved by him, shall be returned and proceeded on as in the case of a bill	1	7	3
The executive power shall be vested in a	2	1	1
He shall hold his office during the term of four years	2	1	1
In case of the removal of the President from office, or of his death, resignation, or inability to discharge the duties of his office, the Vice President shall perform the duties of	2	1	5
[Amendments]	25	------	------
Congress may declare, by law, in the case of the removal, death, resignation, or inability of the President, what officer shall act as	2	1	6
[Amendments]	25	------	------
The President shall receive a compensation which shall not be increased nor diminished during his term, not shall he receive any other emolument from the United States	2	1	6

[1] Article of original Constitution or of amendment.

	Article[1]	Section	Clause
President of the United States—Continued			
Before he enters upon the execution of his office he shall take an oath of office	2	1	7
Shall be commander in chief of the Army and Navy and of the militia of the States when called into actual service	2	2	1
He may require the opinion, in writing, of the principal officer in each of the Executive Departments	2	2	1
He may grant reprieves or pardons for offenses, except in cases of impeachment	2	2	1
He may make treaties by and with the advice and consent of the Senate, two-thirds of the Senators present concurring	2	2	2
He may appoint, by and with the advice and consent of the Senate, ambassadors, other public ministers and consuls, judges of the Supreme Court, and all other officers whose appointments may be authorized by law and not herein provided for	2	2	2
Congress may vest the appointment of inferior officers in the	2	2	2
He may fill up all vacancies that may happen in the recess of the Senate by commissions which shall expire at the end of their next session	2	2	3
He shall give information to Congress of the state of the Union, and recommend measures	2	3	------
On extraordinary occasions he may convene both Houses or either	2	3	------
In case of disagreement between the two Houses as to the time of adjournment, he may adjourn them to such time as he may think proper	2	3	------
He shall receive ambassadors and other public ministers	2	3	------
He shall take care that the laws be faithfully executed	2	3	------
He shall commission all the officers of the United States	2	3	------
On impeachment for, and conviction of, treason, bribery, or other high crimes and misdemeanors, shall be removed from office. The	2	4	------
No person except a natural-born citizen, or a citizen of the United States at the adoption of the Constitution, shall be eligible to the office of	2	1	4
No person shall be elected to office more than twice. [Amendments]	22	------	------
No person who shall not have attained the age of thirty-five years and been fourteen years a resident of the United States shall be eligible to the office of	2	1	4
President and Vice President. Manner of choosing. Each State by its legislature, shall appoint a number of electors equal to the whole number of Senators and Representatives to which the State may be entitled in the Congress	2	1	2
No. Senator or Representative or person holding an office of trust or profit under the United States shall be an elector	2	1	2
Congress may determine the time of choosing the electors and the day on which they shall give their votes, which day shall be the same throughout the United States	2	1	3

[1] Article of original Constitution or of amendment.

Index to the Constitution—Continued

	Article [1]	Section	Clause
President and Vice President—Continued			
The electors shall meet in their respective States and vote by ballot for President and Vice President, one of whom, at least, shall not be an inhabitant of the same State with themselves. [Amendments]	12		
They shall name in distinct ballots the person voted for as President and the person voted for as Vice President. [Amendments]	12		
They shall make distinct lists of the persons voted for as President and as Vice President, which they shall sign and certify and transmit sealed to the President of the Senate at the seat of government. [Amendments]	12		
The President of the Senate shall, in the presence of the Senate and House of Representatives, open all the certificates, and the votes shall then be counted. [Amendments]	12		
The person having the greatest number of votes shall be the President, if such number be a majority of the whole number of electors appointed. [Amendments]	12		
If no person have such majority, then from the persons having the highest numbers, not exceeding three, on the list of those voted for as President, the House of Representatives shall choose immediately, by ballot, the President. [Amendments]	12		
In choosing the President, the votes shall be taken by States, the representation from each State having one vote. [Amendments]	12		
A quorum for this purpose shall consist of a member or members from two-thirds of the States, and a majority of all the States shall be necessary to a choice. [Amendments]	12		
But if no choice shall be made before the 4th of March next following, then the Vice President shall act as President, as in the case of the death or disability of the President. [Amendments]	12		
District of Columbia shall appoint a number of electors equal to the whole number of Senators and Representatives in Congress which the District would be entitled to if it were a State. [Amendments]	23	1	
President of the Senate, but shall have no vote unless the Senate be equally divided. The Vice President shall be	1	3	4
President pro tempore. In the absence of the Vice President the Senate shall choose a	1	3	5
When the Vice President shall exercise the office of President of the United States, the Senate shall choose a	1	3	5
Press. Congress shall pass no law abridging the freedom of speech or of the. [Amendments]	1		
Previous condition of servitude. The right of citizens of the United States to vote shall not be denied or abridged by the United States, or by any State on account of race, color, or. [Amendments]	15	1	

[1] Article of original Constitution or of amendment.

	Article [1]	Section	Clause
Primary elections. The right of citizens of the United State to vote in shall not be denied or abridged by the United States or any State by reason of failure to pay any poll tax or other tax. [Amendments]_____	24	1	_____
Private property shall not be taken for public use without just compensation. [Amendments]_____	5	_____	_____
Privilege. Senators and Representatives shall, in all cases except treason, felony, and breach of the peace, be privileged from arrest during their attendance at the session of their respective Houses, and in going to and returning from the same_____	1	6	1
They shall not be questioned for any speech or debate in either House in any other place_____	1	6	1
Privileges and immunities of citizens of the United States. The citizens of each State shall be entitled to all the privileges and immunities of the citizens of the several States_____	4	2	1
No soldier shall be quartered in any house without the consent of the owner in time of peace. [Amendments]_____	3	_____	_____
No person shall be twice put in jeopardy of life and limb for the same offense. [Amendments]_____	5	_____	_____
All persons born or naturalized in the United States, and subject to the jurisdiction thereof, are citizens of the United States and of the State in which they reside. [Amendments]_____	14	1	_____
No State shall make or enforce any law which shall abridge the privileges or immunities of citizens of the United States. [Amendments]_____	14	1	___·__
No State shall deprive any person of life, liberty, or property without due process of law. [Amendments]_____	14	1	_____
Nor deny to any person within its jurisdiction the equal protection of its laws. [Amendments]_____	14	1	_____
Prizes captured on land or water. Congress shall make rules concerning_____	1	8	11
Probable cause. The right of the people to be secure in their persons, houses, papers, and effects, against unreasonable searches and seizures, shall not be violated. And no warrant shall issue for such but upon. [Amendments]_____	4	_____	_____
Process of law. No person shall be compelled in any criminal case to be a witness against himself, nor be deprived of life, liberty, or property, without due. [Amendments]_____	5	_____	_____
No State shall deprive any person of life, liberty, or property, without due. [Amendments]_____	14	1	_____
Process for obtaining witnesses in his favor. In all criminal prosecutions the accused shall have. [Amendments]_	6	_____	_____
Progress of science and useful arts. Congress shall have power to promote the_____	1	8	8
Property of the United States. Congress may dispose of and make all needful rules and regulations respecting the territory or_____	4	3	2
Property, without due process of law. No person shall be compelled in any criminal case to be a witness against himself; nor shall he be deprived of his life, liberty, or. [Amendments]_____	5	_____	_____
No State shall abridge the privileges or immunities of citizens of the United States; nor deprive any person of his life, liberty, or. [Amendments]_____	14	1	_____

[1] Article of original Constitution or of amendment.

	Article [1]	Section	Clause
Prosecutions. The accused shall have a speedy and public trial in all criminal. [Amendments]	6		
He shall be tried by a jury in the State or district where the crime was committed. [Amendments]	6		
He shall be informed of the nature and cause of the accusation. [Amendments]	6		
He shall be confronted with the witnesses against him. [Amendments]	6		
He shall have compulsory process for obtaining witnesses. [Amendments]	6		
He shall have counsel for his defense. [Amendments]	6		
Protection of the laws. No State shall deny to any person within its jurisdiction the equal. [Amendments]	14	1	
Public debt of the United States incurred in suppressing insurrection or rebellion shall not be questioned. The validity of the. [Amendments]	14	4	
Public safety may require it. The writ of habeas corpus shall not be suspended, unless when in cases of rebellion or invasion the	1	9	2
Public trial by jury. In all criminal prosecutions the accused shall have a speedy and. [Amendments]	6		
Public use. Private property shall not be taken for, without just compensation. [Amendments]	5		
Punishment according to law. Judgment in cases of impeachment shall not extend further than to removal from, and disqualification for, office; but the party convicted shall nevertheless be liable and subject to indictment, trial, judgment, and	1	3	7
Punishments inflicted. Excessive bail shall not be required nor excessive fines imposed nor cruel and unusual. [Amendments]	8		

Q

Qualification for office. No religious test shall ever be required as a	6		3
Qualifications of electors of members of the House of Representatives shall be the same as electors for the most numerous branch of the State legislature	1	2	1
Qualifications of electors of Senators shall be the same as electors of the most numerous branch of the State legislature. [Amendments]	17	1	
Qualifications of members of the House of Representatives. They shall be twenty-five years of age, seven years a citizen of the United States, and an inhabitant of the State in which chosen	1	2	2
Of Senators. They shall be thirty years of age, nine years a citizen of the United States, and an inhabitant of the State in which chosen	1	3	3
Of its own members. Each House shall be the judge of the election, returns, and	1	5	1
Of the President. No person except a natural-born citizen, or a citizen of the United States at the time of the adoption of the Constitution, shall be eligible to the office of President	2	1	4
Neither shall any person be eligible to the office of President who shall not have attained the age of thirty-five years and been fourteen years a resident within the United States	2	1	4
Of the Vice President. No person constitutionally ineligible to the office of President shall be eligible to that of Vice President. [Amendments]	12		

[1] Article of original Constitution or of amendment.

	Article [1]	Section	Clause
Quartered in any house without the consent of the owner in time of peace. No soldier shall be. [Amendments]	3		
Quorum to do business. A majority of each House shall constitute a	1	5	1
But a smaller number than a quorum may adjourn from day to day and may be authorized to compel the attendance of absent members	1	5	1
Of the House of Representatives for choosing a President shall consist of a member or members from two-thirds of the States, and a majority of all the States shall be necessary to a choice. [Amendments]	12		
Quorum to elect a Vice President by the Senate. Two-thirds of the whole number of Senators shall be a. [Amendments]	12		
A majority of the whole number shall be necessary to a choice. [Amendments]	12		

R

	Article [1]	Section	Clause
Race, color, or previous condition of servitude. The right of citizens of the United States to vote shall not be denied or abridged by the United States or by any State on account of. [Amendments]	15	1	
Ratification of amendments to the Constitution shall be by the legislatures of three-fourths of the several States or by conventions in three-fourths of the States, accordingly as Congress may propose	5		
Ratification of the conventions of nine States shall be sufficient to establish the Constitution between the States so ratifying the same	7		
Ratio of representation until the first enumeration under the Constitution shall be made not to exceed one for every thirty thousand	1	2	3
Ratio of representation shall be apportioned among the several States according to their respective numbers, counting the whole number of persons in each State, excluding Indians not taxed. [Amendments]	14	2	
But when the right to vote for Presidential electors or members of Congress, or the legislative, executive, and judicial officers of the State, except for engaging in rebellion or other crime, shall be denied or abridged by a State, the basis of representation shall be reduced therein in the proportion of such denial or abridgement of the right to vote. [Amendments]	14	2	
Rebellion against the United States. Persons who, while holding certain Federal and State offices, took an oath to support the Constitution, afterward engaged in insurrection or rebellion, disabled from holding office under the United States. [Amendments]	14	3	
But Congress may by a vote of two-thirds of each House remove such disability. [Amendments]	14	3	
Rebellion against the United States. Debts incurred for pensions and bounties for services in suppressing the rebellion shall not be questioned. [Amendments]	14	4	
All debts and obligations incurred in aid of the rebellion, and all claims for the loss or emancipation of slaves, declared and held to be illegal and void. [Amendments]	14	4	

[1] Article of original Constitution or of amendment.

	Article [1]	Section	Clause
Rebellion or invasion. The writ of habeas corpus shall not be suspended except when the public safety may require it in cases of	1	9	2
Receipts and expenditures of all public money shall be published from time to time. A regular statement of	1	9	7
Recess of the Senate. The President may grant commissions, which shall expire at the end of the next session, to fill vacancies that may happen during the	2	2	3
Reconsideration of a bill returned by the President with his objections. Proceedings to be had upon the	1	7	2
Records, and judicial proceedings of every other State. Full faith and credit shall be given in each State to the acts	4	1	------
Congress shall prescribe the manner of proving such acts, records, and proceedings	4	1	------
Redress of grievances. Congress shall make no law abridging the right of the people peaceably to assemble and to petitions for the. [Amendments]	1	------	------
Regulations, except as to the places of choosing Senators. The time, places, and manner of holding elections for Senators and Representatives shall be prescribed by the legislatures of the States, but Congress may at any time by law make or alter such	1	4	1
Regulations of commerce or revenue. Preference to the ports of one State over those of another shall not be given by any	1	9	6
Religion or prohibiting the free exercise thereof. Congress shall make no law respecting the establishment of. [Amendments]	1	------	------
Religious tests shall ever be required as a qualification for any office or public trust under the United States. No	6	------	3
Removal of the President from office, the same shall devolve on the Vice President. In case of the	2	1	5
[Amendments]	25	------	------
Representation. No State, without its consent, shall be deprived of its equal suffrage in the Senate	5	------	------
Representation and direct taxation, how apportioned among the several States	1	2	3
Representation until the first enumeration under the Constitution not to exceed one for every thirty thousand. The ratio of	1	2	3
Representation in any State. The executive thereof shall issue writs of election to fill vacancies in the	1	2	4
Representation among the several States shall be according to their respective numbers, counting the whole number of persons in each State, excluding Indians not taxed. The ratio of. [Amendments]	14	2	------
But where the right to vote in certain Federal and State elections is abridged for any cause other than rebellion or other crime, the basis of representation shall be reduced. [Amendments]	14	2	------
Representatives. Congress shall consist of a Senate and House of	1	1	------
Qualifications of electors of members of the House of	1	2	1
No person shall be a Representative who shall not have attained the age of twenty-five years, been seven years a citizen of the United States, and an inhabitant of the State in which he shall be chosen	1	2	2
And direct taxes, how apportioned among the several States	1	2	3

[1] Article of original Constitution or of amendment.

	Article [1]	Section	Clause
Representatives—Continued			
Executives of the States shall issue writs of election to fill vacancies in the House of_____	1	2	4
Shall choose their Speaker and other officers. The House of_____	1	2	5
Shall have the sole power of impeachment. The House of_____	1	2	5
The times, places, and manner of choosing Representatives shall be prescribed by the legislatures of the States_____	1	4	1
But Congress may make by law at any time or alter such regulations except as to the places of choosing Senators_____	1	4	1
And Senators shall receive a compensation, to be ascertained by law_____	1	6	1
Shall in all cases, except treason, felony, and breach of the peace, be privileged from arrest during attendance at the session of the House, and in going to and returning from the same_____	1	6	1
Shall not be questioned in any other place for any speech or debate. Members of the House of_____	1	6	1
No member shall be appointed during his term to any civil office which shall have been created, or the emoluments of which shall have been increased, during such term_____	1	6	2
No person holding any office under the United States shall, while holding such office be a member of the House of_____	1	6	2
All bills for raising revenue shall originate in the House of_____	1	7	1
No Senator or Representative shall be an elector for President or Vice President_____	2	1	2
Representatives shall be bound by an oath or affirmation to support the Constitution of the United States. The Senators and_____	6	------	3
Representatives among the several States. Provisions relative to the apportionment of. [Amendments]_____	14	2	------
Representatives and Senators. Prescribing certain disqualifications for office as. [Amendments]_____	14	3	------
But Congress may, by a vote of two-thirds of each House remove such disqualification. [Amendments]_	14	3	------
Reprieves and pardons except in cases of impeachment. The President may grant_____	2	2	1
Reprisal. Congress shall have power to grant letters of marque and_____	1	8	11
No State shall grant any letters of marque and_____	1	10	1
Republican form of government. The United States shall guarantee to every State in this Union a_____	4	4	------
Republican form of government. And shall protect each of them against invasion; and on the application of the legislature, or of the executive (when the legislature cannot be convened), against domestic violence_____	4	4	------
Reserved rights of the States and the people. The enumeration in the Constitution of certain rights shall not be construed to deny or disparage others retained by the people. [Amendments]_____	9	------	------
The powers not delegated to the United States by the Constitution, nor prohibited by it to the States, are reserved to the States respectively, or to the people. [Amendments]_____	10	------	------

[1] Article of original Constitution or of amendment.

	Article [1]	Section	Clause
Resignation, or inability of the President, the duties and powers of his office shall devolve on the Vice President. In case of the death_____	2	1	5
[Amendments]_____	25		
Resignation, or inability of the President. Congress may by law provide for the case of the removal, death_____	2	1	5
[Amendments]_____	25		
Resolution, or vote (except on a question of adjournment) requiring the concurrence of the two Houses shall before it becomes a law, be presented to the President. Every order_____	1	7	3
Revenue shall originate in the House of Representatives. All bills for raising_____	1	7	1
Revenue. Preference shall not be given to the ports of one State over those of another by any regulations of commerce or_____	1	9	6
Rhode Island entitled to one Representative in the first Congress_____	1	2	3
Right of petition. Congress shall make no law abridging the right of the people peaceably to assemble and to petition for the redress of grievances. [Amendments]_____	1		
Right to keep and bear arms. A well-regulated militia being necessary to the security of a free State, the right of the people to keep and bear arms shall not be infringed. [Amendments]_____	2		
Rights in the Constitution shall not be construed to deny or disparage others retained by the people. The enumeration of certain. [Amendments]_____	9		
Rights not delegated to the United States nor prohibited to the States are reserved to the States or to the people. [Amendments]_____	10		
Rules of its proceedings. Each House may determine the_	1	5	2
Rules and regulations respecting the territory or other property of the United States. Congress shall dispose of and make all needful_____	4	3	2
Rules of the common law. All suits involving over twenty dollars shall be tried by jury according to the. [Amendments]_____	7		
No fact tried by a jury shall be re-examined except according to the. [Amendments]_____	7		

S

	Article [1]	Section	Clause
Science and the useful arts by securing to authors and inventors the exclusive right to their writings and discoveries. Congress shall have power to promote the progress of_____	1	8	8
Searches and seizures shall not be violated. The right of the people to be secure against unreasonable. [Amendments]_____	4		
And no warrants shall be issued but upon probable causes, on oath or affirmation, describing the place to be searched and the persons or things to be seized. [Amendments]_____	4		
Seat of Government. Congress shall exercise exclusive legislation in all cases over such district as may become the_____	1	8	17
Securities and current coin of the United States. Congress shall provide for punishing the counterfeiting of the_____	1	8	6

[1] Article of original Constitution or of amendment.

	Article [1]	Section	Clause
Security of a free State, the right of the people to keep and bear arms shall not be infringed. A well-regulated militia being necessary to the. [Amendments]_____	2	_____	_____
Senate and House of Representatives. The Congress of the United States shall consist of a_____	1	1	_____
Senate of the United States. The Senate shall be composed of two Senators from each State chosen by the legislature for six years_____	1	3	1
The Senate shall be composed of two Senators from each State, elected by the people thereof, for six years. [Amendments]_____	17	1	_____
Qualifications of electors of Senators. [Amendments]__	17	1	_____
If vacancies happen during the recess of the legislature of a State, the executive thereof may make temporary appointments until the next meeting of the legislature_____	1	3	2
When vacancies happen the executive authority of the State shall issue writs of election to fill such vacancies; provided, that the legislature of any State may empower the executive thereof to make temporary appointment until the people fill the vacancies by election as the legislature may direct. [Amendments]_____	17	2	_____
The Vice President shall be President of the Senate, but shall have no vote unless the Senate be equally divided_____	1	3	4
The Senate shall choose their other officers, and also a President pro tempore in the absence of the Vice President or when he shall exercise the office of President_____	1	3	5
The Senate shall have the sole power to try all impeachments. When sitting for that purpose they shall be on oath or affirmation_____	1	3	6
When the President of the United States is tried the Chief Justice shall preside; and no person shall be convicted without the concurrence of two-thirds of the members present_____	1	3	6
It shall be the judge of the elections, returns, and qualifications of its own members_____	1	5	1
A majority shall constitute a quorum to do business, but a smaller number may adjourn from day to day, and may be authorized to compel the attendance of absent members_____	1	5	1
It may determine the rules of its proceedings, punish a member for disorderly behavior, and with the concurrence of two-thirds expel a member_____	1	5	2
It shall keep a journal of its proceedings and from time to time publish the same, except such parts as may in their judgment require secrecy_____	1	5	3
It shall not adjourn for more than three days during a session without the consent of the other House___	1	5	4
It may propose amendments to bills for raising revenue, but such bills shall originate in the House of Representatives_____	1	7	1
The Senate shall advise and consent to the ratification of all treaties, provided two-thirds of the members present concur_____	2	2	2

[1] Article of original Constitution or of amendment.

	Article [1]	Section	Clause
Senate of the United States—Continued			
It shall advise and consent to the appointment of ambassadors, other public ministers and consuls, judges of the Supreme Court, and all other officers not herein otherwise provided for_____	2	2	2
It may be convened by the President on extraordinary occasions_____	2	3	1
No State, without its consent, shall be deprived of its equal suffrage in the Senate_____	5	_____	_____
Senators. They shall, immediately after assembling, under their first election, be divided into three classes, so that the seats of one-third shall become vacant at the expiration of every second year_____	1	3	2
No person shall be a Senator who shall not be thirty years of age, nine years a citizen of the United States, and an inhabitant when elected of the State for which he shall be chosen_____	1	3	3
The times, places, and manner of choosing Senators may be fixed by the legislature of a State, but Congress may by law make or alter such regulations, except as to the places of choosing_____	1	4	1
If vacancies happen during the recess of the legislature of a State, the executive thereof may make temporary appointments until the next meeting of the legislature_____	1	3	2
If vacancies happen the executive authority of the State shall issue writs of election to fill such vacancies; provided, that the legislature of any State may empower the executive thereof to make temporary appointment until the people fill the vacancies by election as the legislature may direct. [Amendments]_____	17	2	_____
They shall in all cases, except treason, felony, and breach of the peace, be privileged from arrest during their attendance at the session of the Senate and in going to and returning from the same_____	1	6	1
Senators and Representatives shall receive a compensation to be ascertained by law_____	1	6	1
Senators and Representatives shall not be questioned for any speech or debate in either House in any other place_____	1	6	1
No Senator or Representative shall, during the time for which he was elected, be appointed to any civil office under the United States which shall have been created, or of which the emoluments shall have been increased, during such term_____	1	6	2
No person holding any office under the United States shall be a member of either House during his continuance in office_____	1	6	2
No Senator or Representative or person holding an office of trust or profit under the United States shall be an elector for President and Vice President_____	2	1	2
Senators and Representatives shall be bound by an oath or affirmation to support the Constitution____	6	_____	3
No person shall be a Senator or Representative who, having, as a Federal or State officer, taken an oath to support the Constitution, afterward engaged in rebellion against the United States. [Amendments]_	14	3	_____
But Congress may, by a vote of two-thirds of each House, remove such disability. [Amendments]____	14	3	_____

[1] Article of original Constitution or of amendment.

	Article [1]	Section	Clause
Service or labor in one State, escaping into another State, shall be delivered up to the party to whom such service or labor may be due. Fugitives from_____	4	2	3
Servitude, except as a punishment for crime, whereof the party shall have been duly convicted, shall exist in the United States or any place subject to their jurisdiction. Neither slavery nor involuntary. [Amendments]_____	13	1	_____
Servitude. The right of citizens of the United States to vote shall not be denied or abridged by the United States or by any State, on account of race, color, or previous condition of. [Amendments]_____	15	1	_____
Sex. Right of citizens to vote shall not be denied or abridged by the United States or any State on account of sex. [Amendments]_____	19	_____	_____
Ships of war in time of peace, without the consent of Congress. No State shall keep troops or_____	1	10	3
Silver coin a tender in payment of debts. No State shall make anything but gold and_____	1	10	1
Slave. Neither the United States nor any State shall assume or pay any debt or obligation incurred in aid of insurrection or rebellion, or any claim for the loss or emancipation of any. [Amendments]_____	14	4	_____
Slavery nor involuntary servitude, except as a punishment for crime, whereof the party shall have been duly convicted, shall exist in the United States, or any places subject to their jurisdiction. Neither. [Amendments]_	13	1	_____
Soldiers shall not be quartered, in time of peace, in any house without the consent of the owner. [Amendments]_	3	_____	_____
South Carolina entitled to five Representatives in the first Congress_____	1	2	3
Speaker and other officers. The House of Representatives shall choose their_____	1	2	5
Speech or of the press. Congress shall make no law abridging the freedom of. [Amendments]_____	1	_____	_____
Speedy and public trial by a jury. In all criminal prosecutions the accused shall have a. [Amendments]_____	6	_____	_____
Standard of weights and measures. Congress shall fix the_	1	8	5
State of the Union. The President shall, from time to time, give Congress information of the_____	2	3	_____
State legislatures, and all executive and judicial officers of the United States, shall take an oath to support the Constitution. All members of the several_____	6	_____	3
States. When vacancies happen in the representation from any State, the executive authority shall issue writs of election to fill such vacancies_____	1	2	4
When vacancies happen in the representation of any State in the Senate, the executive authority shall issue writs of election to fill vacancies. [Amendments]_____	17	2	_____
Congress shall have power to regulate commerce among the several_____	1	8	3
No State shall enter into any treaty, alliance, or confederation_____	1	10	1
Shall not grant letters of marque and reprisal_____	1	10	1
Shall not coin money_____	1	10	1
Shall not emit bills of credit_____	1	10	1
Shall not make anything but gold and silver coin a tender in payment of debts_____	1	10	1

[1] Article of original Constitution or of amendment.

	Article [1]	Section	Clause
States. When vacancies—Continued			
Shall not pass any bill of attainder, ex post facto law, or law impairing the obligation of contracts_____	1	10	1
Shall not grant any title of nobility_____	1	10	1
Shall not, without the consent of Congress, lay any duties on imports or exports, except what may be absolutely necessary for executing its inspection laws_____	1	10	2
Shall not, without the consent of Congress, lay any duty of tonnage, keep troops or ships of war in time of peace, enter into any agreement or compact with another State or with a foreign power, or engage in war unless actually invaded or in such imminent danger as will not admit of delay_____	1	10	3
Full faith and credit in every other State shall be given to the public acts, records, and judicial proceedings of each State_____	4	1	------
Congress shall prescribe the manner of proving such acts, records, and proceedings_____	4	1	------
Citizens of each State shall be entitled to all privileges and immunities of citizens in the several States____	4	2	1
New States may be admitted by Congress into this Union_____	4	3	1
But no new State shall be formed or erected within the jurisdiction of another State_____	4	3	1
Nor any State formed by the junction of two or more States or parts of States, without the consent of the legislatures as well as of Congress_____	4	3	1
No State shall be deprived, without its consent, of its equal suffrage in the Senate_____	5	------	------
Three-fourths of the legislatures of the States, or conventions of three-fourths of the States, as Congress shall prescribe, may ratify amendments to the Constitution_____	5	------	------
The United States shall guarantee a republican form of government to every State in the Union_____	4	4	------
They shall protect each State against invasion_____	4	4	------
And on application of the legislature, or the executive (when the legislature cannot be convened), against domestic violence_____	4	4	------
The ratification by nine States shall be sufficient to establish the Constitution between the States so ratifying the same_____	7	------	------
When the choice of President shall devolve on the House of Representatives, the vote shall be taken by States. [Amendments]_____	12	------	------
But in choosing the President the vote shall be taken by States, the representation from each State having one vote. [Amendments]_____	12	------	------
A quorum for choice of President shall consist of a member or members from two-thirds of the States, and a majority of all the States shall be necessary to a choice. [Amendments]_____	12	------	------
States or the people. Powers not delegated to the United States, nor prohibited to the States, are reserved to the. [Amendments]_____	10	------	------
Suffrage in the Senate. No State shall be deprived without its consent of its equal_____	5	------	------
No denial of right to vote on account of sex. [Amendments]_____	19	------	------

[1] Article of original Constitution or of amendment.

	Article [1]	Section	Clause
Suits at common law, where the value in controversy shall exceed $20, shall be tried by jury. [Amendments]	7		
In law or equity against one of the States, by citizens of another State, or by citizens of a foreign State. The judicial power of the United States shall not extend to. [Amendments]	11		
Supreme Court. Congress shall have power to constitute tribunals inferior to the	1	8	9
Supreme Court, and such inferior courts as Congress may establish. The judicial power of the United States shall be vested in one	3	1	
Supreme Court. The judges of the Supreme and inferior courts shall hold their offices during good behavior	3	1	
The compensation of the judges shall not be diminished during their continuance in office	3	1	
Shall have original jurisdiction. In all cases affecting ambassadors, other public ministers and consuls, and in which a State may be a party, the	3	2	2
Shall have appellate jurisdiction, both as to law and the fact, with such exceptions and regulations as Congress may make. The	3	2	2
Supreme law of the land. This Constitution, the laws made in pursuance thereof, and the treaties of the United States, shall be the	6		2
The judges in every State shall be bound thereby	6		2
Suppress insurrections and repel invasions. Congress shall provide for calling forth the militia to execute the laws	1	8	15
Suppression of insurrection or rebellion shall not be questioned. The public debt, including the debt for pensions and bounties, incurred in the. [Amendments]	14	4	

T

	Article [1]	Section	Clause
Tax shall be laid unless in proportion to the census or enumeration. No capitation or other direct	1	9	4
Tax on incomes authorized without apportionment among the several States, and without regard to any census or enumeration. [Amendments]	16		
Tax or duty shall be laid on articles exported from any State. No	1	9	5
Tax. The right of citizens of the United States to vote shall not be denied or abridged by the United States or any State by reason of failure to pay. [Amendments]	24	1	
Taxes (direct) and Representatives, how apportioned among the several States	1	2	3
Taxes, duties, imposts, and excises. Congress shall have power to lay	1	8	1
They shall be uniform throughout the United States	1	8	1
Temporary appointments until the next meeting of the legislature. If vacancies happen in the Senate in the recess of the legislature of a State, the executive of the State shall make	1	3	2
Tender in payment of debts. No State shall make anything but gold and silver coin a	1	10	1
Terms of four years. The President and Vice President shall hold their offices for the	2	1	1
Term of office. President, not more than twice. [Amendments]	22		
Term for which he is elected. No Senator or Representative shall be appointed to any office under the United States which shall have been created or its emoluments increased during the	1	6	2

[1] Article of original Constitution or of amendment.

	Article[1]	Section	Clause
Territory or other property of the United States. Congress shall dispose of and make all needful rules and regulations respecting the	4	3	2
Test as a qualification for any office or public trust shall ever be required. No religious	6	------	3
Testimony of two witnesses to the same overt act, or on confession in open court. No person shall be convicted of treason except on the	3	3	1
Three-fourths of the legislatures of the States, or conventions in three-fourths of the States, as Congress shall prescribe, may ratify amendments to the Constitution	5	------	------
Tie. The Vice President shall have no vote unless the Senate be equally divided	1	3	4
Times, places, and manner of holding elections for Senators and Representatives shall be prescribed in each State by the legislature thereof	1	4	1
But Congress may at any time by law make or alter such regulations, except as to the places of choosing Senators	1	4	1
Title of nobility. The United States shall not grant any	1	9	8
No State shall grant any	1	10	1
Title of any kind, from any king, prince, or foreign state, without the consent of Congress. No person holding any office under the United States shall accept of any	1	9	8
Tonnage without the consent of Congress. No State shall lay any duty of	1	10	3
Tranquility, provide for the common defense, &c. To insure domestic. [Preamble]	------	------	------
Treason shall consist only in levying war against the United States, or in adhering to their enemies, giving them aid and comfort	3	3	1
No person shall, unless on the testimony of two witnesses to the same overt act, or on confession in open court, be convicted of	3	3	1
Congress shall have power to declare the punishment of	3	3	2
Shall not work corruption of blood. Attainder of	3	3	2
Shall not work forfeiture, except during the life of the person attained. Attainder of	3	3	2
Treason, bribery, or other high crimes and misdemeanors. The President, Vice President, and all civil officers shall be removed from office on impeachment for and conviction of	2	4	1
Treason, felony, and breach of the peace. Senators and Representatives shall be privileged from arrest while attending or while going to or returning from the sessions of Congress, except in cases of	1	6	1
Treasury, but in consequence of appropriations made by law. No money shall be drawn from the	1	9	7
Treaties. The President shall have power, with the advice and consent of the Senate, provided two-thirds of the Senators present concur, to make	2	2	2
The judicial power shall extend to all cases arising under the Constitution, laws, and	3	2	1
They shall be the supreme law of the land, and the judges in every State shall be bound thereby	6	------	2
Treaty, alliance, or confederation. No State shall enter into any	1	10	1
Trial, judgment, and punishment according to law. Judgment in cases of impeachment shall not extend further than to removal from, and disqualification for, office; but the party convicted shall nevertheless be liable and subject to indictment	1	3	7

[1] Article of original Constitution or of amendment.

	Article [1]	Section	Clause
Trial by jury. All crimes, except in cases of impeachment, shall be tried by jury	3	2	3
Such trial shall be held in the State within which the crime shall have been committed	3	2	3
But when not committed within a State, the trial shall be at such a place as Congress may by law have directed	3	2	3
In all criminal prosecutions the accused shall have a speedy and public. [Amendments]	6		
Suits at common law, when the amount exceeds $20, shall be by. [Amendments]	7		
Tribunals inferior to the Supreme Court. Congress shall have power to constitute	1	8	9
Troops or ships of war in time of peace without the consent of Congress. No State shall keep	1	10	3
Trust or profit under the United States, shall be an elector for President and Vice President. No Senator, Representative, or person holding any office of	2	1	2
Two-thirds of the members present. No person shall be convicted on an impeachment without the concurrence of	1	3	6
Two-thirds, may expel a member. Each House, with the concurrence of	1	5	2
Two-thirds. A bill returned by the President with his objections, may be repassed by each House by a vote of	1	7	2
Two-thirds of the Senators present concur. The President shall have power, by and with the advice and consent of the Senate, to make treaties, provided	2	2	2
Two-thirds of the legislatures of the several States. Congress shall call a convention for proposing amendments to the Constitution on the application of	5		
Two-thirds of both Houses shall deem it necessary. Congress shall propose amendments to the Constitution whenever	5		
Two-thirds of the States. When the choice of a President shall devolve on the House of Representatives, a quorum shall consist of a member or members from. [Amendments]	12		
Two-thirds of the whole number of Senators. A quorum of the Senate, when choosing a Vice-President, shall consist of. [Amendments]	12		
Two-thirds, may remove the disabilities imposed by the third section of the fourteenth amendment. Congress, by a vote of. [Amendments]	14	3	
Two years. Appropriations for raising and supporting armies shall not be for a longer term than	1	8	12

U

	Article [1]	Section	Clause
Union. To establish a more perfect. [Preamble]			
The President shall, from time to time, give to Congress information of the state of the	2	3	1
New States may be admitted by Congress into this	4	3	1
But no new States shall be formed or erected within the jurisdiction of another	4	3	1
Unreasonable searches and seizures. The people shall be secured in their persons, houses, papers, and effects against. [Amendments]	4		
And no warrants shall be issued but upon probable cause, supported by oath or affirmation, and particularly describing the place to be searched, and the persons or things to be seized. [Amendments]	4		

[1] Article of original Constitution or of amendment.

	Article [1]	Section	Clause
Unusual punishments inflicted. Excessive bail shall not be required, nor excessive fines imposed, nor cruel and. [Amendments]	8		
Use without just compensation. Private property shall not be taken for public. [Amendments]	5		
Useful arts, by securing for limited times to authors and inventors the exclusive right to their writings and inventions. Congress shall have power to promote the progress of science and the	1	8	8

V

	Article [1]	Section	Clause
Vacancies happening in the representation of a State. The executive thereof shall issue writs of election to fill	1	2	4
Vacancies happening in the representation of a State in the Senate. The executive thereof shall issue writs of election to fill. [Amendments]	17	2	
Vacancies happening in the Senate in the recess of the legislature of a State. How filled	1	3	2
Vacancies that happen during the recess of the Senate, by granting commissions which shall expire at the end of the next session. The President shall have power to fill.	2	2	3
Validity of the public debt incurred in suppressing insurrection against the United States, including debt for pensions and bounties, shall not be questioned. [Amendments]	14	4	
Vessels bound to or from the ports of one State, shall not be obliged to enter, clear, or pay duties in another State	1	9	6
Veto of a bill by the President. Proceedings of the two Houses upon the	1	7	2
Vice President of the United States shall be President of the Senate	1	3	4
He shall have no vote unless the Senate be equally divided	1	3	4
The Senate shall choose a President pro tempore in the absence of the	1	3	5
He shall be chosen for the term of four years	2	1	1
The number and the manner of appointing electors for President and	2	1	2
In case of the removal, death, resignation, or inability of the President, the powers and duties of his office shall devolve on the	2	1	5
[Amendments]	25		
Congress may provide by law for the case of the removal, death, resignation, or inability both of the President and	2	1	5
[Amendments]	25		
On impeachment for and conviction of treason, bribery, and other high crimes and misdemeanors, shall be removed from office. The	2	4	
Vice President. The manner of choosing the. The electors shall meet in their respective States and vote by ballot for President and Vice President, one of whom, at least, shall not be an inhabitant of the same State with themselves. [Amendments]	12		
Additional provision for succession through act of Congress. [Amendments]	20	4	
Nomination by President in case of vacancy in office. [Amendments]	25	2	

[1] Article of original Constitution or of amendment.

	Article [1]	Section	Clause
Vice President. The manner of choosing—Continued			
Term of office, beginning and ending. [Amendments]	20	1	_____
The electors shall name, in distinct ballots, the person voted for as Vice President. [Amendments]	12	_____	_____
They shall make distinct lists of the persons voted for as Vice President, which lists they shall sign and certify, and send sealed to the seat of Government, directed to the President of the Senate. [Amendments]	12	_____	_____
The President of the Senate shall, in the presence of the Senate and House of Representatives, open all the certificates, and the votes shall be then counted. [Amendments]	12	_____	_____
The person having the greatest number of votes shall be Vice President, if such number be a majority of the whole number of electors. [Amendments]	12	_____	_____
If no person have a majority, then from the two highest numbers on the list the Senate shall choose the Vice President. [Amendments]	12	_____	_____
A quorum for this purpose shall consist of two-thirds of the whole number of Senators; and a majority of the whole number shall be necessary to a choice. [Amendments]	12	_____	_____
But if the House shall make no choice of a President before the 4th of March next following, then the Vice President shall act as President, as in the case of the death or other constitutional disability of the President. [Amendments]	12	_____	_____
No person constitutionally ineligble as President shall be eligible as. [Amendments]	12	_____	_____
Vacancy in office of. President shall nominate a Vice President who shall take office upon confirmation by both Houses of Congress. [Amendments]	25	_____	_____
Violence. The United States shall guarantee to every State a republican form of government, and shall protect each State against invasion and domestic	4	4	_____
Virginia entitled to ten Representatives in the first Congress	1	2	3
Vote. Each Senator shall have one	1	3	1
The Vice President, unless the Senate be equally divided, shall have no	1	3	4
Vote requiring the concurrence of the two Houses (except upon a question of adjournment) shall be presented to the President. Every order, resolution, or	1	7	3
Vote, shall not be denied or abridged by the United States or by any State on account of race, color, or previous condition of servitude. The right of citizens of the United States to. [Amendments]	15	1	_____
Vote, shall not be denied or abridged by the United States or any States by reason of failure to pay any poll tax or other tax. The right of citizens of the United States to. [Amendments]	24	1	_____
Vote. Right of citizens who are eighteen years of age or older to vote shall not be denied or abridged by the United States or any State, on account of age. [Amendments]	26	1	_____
Right of citizens to vote shall not be denied or abridged by the United States or any State on account of sex. [Amendments]	19	_____	_____

[1] Article of original Constitution or of amendment.

	Article [1]	Section	Clause
Vote of two-thirds. Each House may expel a member by a__	1	5	2
A bill vetoed by the President may be repassed in each House by a_____	1	7	2
No person shall be convicted on an impeachment except by a_____	1	3	6
Whenever both Houses shall deem it necessary, Congress may propose amendments to the Constitution by a_____	5	-----	-----
The President may make treaties with the advice and consent of the Senate, by a_____	2	2	2
Disabilities incurred by participation in insurrection or rebellion, may be relieved by Congress by a. [Amendments]_____	14	3	-----

W

	Article [1]	Section	Clause
War, grant letters of marque and reprisal, and make rules concerning captures on land and water. Congress shall have power to declare_____	1	8	11
For governing the land and naval forces. Congress shall have power to make rules and articles of_____	1	8	14
No State shall, without the consent of Congress, unless actually invaded, or in such imminent danger as will not admit of delay, engage in_____	1	10	3
War against the United States, adhering to their enemies, and giving them aid and comfort. Treason shall consist only in levying_____	3	3	1
Warrants shall issue but upon probable cause, on oath or affirmation, describing the place to be searched, and the person or things to be seized. No. [Amendments]____	4	-----	-----
Weights and measures. Congress shall fix the standard of_	1	8	5
Welfare and to secure the blessings of liberty, &c. To promote the general. [Preamble]_____	-----	-----	-----
Welfare. Congress shall have power to provide for the common defense and general_____	1	8	1
Witness against himself. No person shall, in a criminal case, be compelled to be a. [Amendments]_____	5	-----	-----
Witnesses against him. In all criminal prosecutions the accused shall be confronted with the. [Amendments]___	6	-----	-----
Witnesses in his favor. In all criminal prosecutions the accused shall have compulsory process for obtaining. [Amendments]_____	6	-----	-----
Witnesses to the same overt act, or on confession in open court. No person shall be convicted of treason unless on the testimony of two_____	3	3	1
Writ of habeas corpus shall not be suspended unless in case of rebellion or invasion the public safety may require it__	1	9	2
Writs of election to fill vacancies in the representation of any State. The executives of the State shall issue_____	1	2	4
Written opinion of the principal officer in each of the Executive Departments on any subject relating to the duties of his office. The President may require the____	2	2	1

Y

	Article [1]	Section	Clause
Yeas and nays of the members of either House shall, at the desire of one-fifth of those present, be entered on the journals_____	1	5	3
The votes of both Houses upon the reconsideration of a bill returned by the President with his objections shall be determined by_____	1	7	2

[1] Article of original Constitution or of amendment.

OFFICIAL SEAL OF THE UNITED STATES OF AMERICA

Front of Great Seal

Reverse of Seal

The unfinished pyramid has 13 steps representing the original colonies. At the top of the pyramid is the all-seeing eye of the Creator. Annuit Coeptis (God has favored our undertaking) appears over the eye of God. Novus Ordo Seclorum (New Order of the Ages) appears at the bottom of the pyramid.